Strengths,
Clarity,
and Focus

STRENGTHS, CLARITY, AND FOCUS

THINKING DIFFERENTLY TO ACHIEVE BREAKTHROUGH RESULTS

JIM TRINKA, PHD

STRENGTHS, CLARITY, AND FOCUS
Thinking Differently to Achieve Breakthrough Results

iUniverse books may be ordered through booksellers or by contacting:

iUniverse
1663 Liberty Drive
Bloomington, IN 47403
www.iuniverse.com
1-800-Authors (1-800-288-4677)

Because of the dynamic nature of the Internet, any web addresses or links contained in this book may have changed since publication and may no longer be valid. The views expressed in this work are solely those of the author and do not necessarily reflect the views of the publisher, and the publisher hereby disclaims any responsibility for them.

Any people depicted in stock imagery provided by Thinkstock are models, and such images are being used for illustrative purposes only. Certain stock imagery © Thinkstock.

ISBN: 978-1-5320-3202-8 (sc)
ISBN: 978-1-5320-3204-2 (hc)
ISBN: 978-1-5320-3203-5 (e)

Library of Congress Control Number: 2017913497

Print information available on the last page.

iUniverse rev. date: 09/14/2017

The significant problems we face cannot be solved at the same level of thinking we were at when we created them.
—Albert Einstein

Recognize your highest calling as early in life as possible. Proactively and creatively persist, day in and day out. Leave an enduring legacy.
—Frank McKinney

You shouldn't focus on why you can't do something, which is what most people do. You should focus on why perhaps you can, and be one of the exceptions.
—Steve Case

Knowing is not enough. We must apply. Willing is not enough. We must do.
—Bruce Lee

Focus on problems, you'll have more problems. When you focus on possibilities, you'll have more opportunities. Dream. Wish. Make it happen.
—Kush and Wizdom

The ageless essence of leadership is to create an alignment of strengths in ways that make a system's weaknesses irrelevant.
—Peter Drucker

True leadership lies in guiding others to success. In ensuring that everyone is performing at their best, doing the work they are pledged to do, and doing it well.
—Bill Owens

When I let go of what I am, I become what I might be.
—Lao Tzu

TABLE OF CONTENTS

TABLE OF FIGURES

CHAPTER 1

INTRODUCTION

Being a leader brings with it a responsibility to do something of significance that makes families, communities, work organizations, nations, the environment, and the world better places than they are today.

—James Kouzes and Barry Posner

Be the change that you want to see in the world.

—Mahatma Gandhi

There may be "born leaders," but there surely are far too few of them to depend on them. Leadership must be learned and can be learned.

—Peter Drucker

An Example

To begin the discussion of the strengths, clarity, and focus approach, I will offer a real life story of a leader who successfully used it to address a challenging situation. Ed, a new executive, had recently taken over an information technology division within a very large financial services

1

organization. His division of about 500 people managed one of only two nationwide computing centers, which hosted about half of the organization's website and gigantic data storage capacity. The division had a long-standing reputation for excessive computer downtime, low productivity, and generally poor customer service and there were rumors that the organization had made a decision to close the center and consolidate computing capacity at the other location. After about six months on the job, Ed faced the choice of recommending closure or implementing a plan to reenergize the organization, vastly improve the division's performance, and change the division's reputation. While many of us might have chosen the former path that offered a politically safer option, Ed chose the latter because he instinctively knew that his people could flourish under improved leadership.

Now came the issue that many of us face—how does one increase both leadership effectiveness and employee performance in minimal time so that corporate management can quickly perceive the improvement? A tall order, to be sure, when considering that, like most of us, Ed could not afford an extensive leadership development effort within the meager resources of his reduced budget. Still, he knew that his thirty existing managers possessed strengths that could change the leadership climate to avoid closure of the center and a layoff of its employees. A recent analysis of 360-degree assessments of all of his managers revealed that they exhibited common strengths in strategic thinking, technical credibility, and developing others. Ed provided clarity to his leadership team that they would focus development efforts on these three areas to best address the challenges they faced. He believed he could leverage these strengths to achieve breakthrough improvements in both overall leadership effectiveness and employee productivity to turn around the organization's performance.

With a clear focus, Ed began a series of one-on-one developmental conversations with his direct reports to begin plans to enhance their leadership capabilities. He created a template for similar discussions that would cascade down through each leadership level. He obtained help from internal consultants to suggest sources of reading, online learning, and course work for his leaders to access in their developmental journey. Ed also identified a coalition of four of his best managers to be mentors. He chose those capable and willing to teach others and closest to demonstrating the enlightened leadership he believed the organization needed to make the next step.

By leveraging strengths, clarifying expectations about leadership focus, and creating a learning environment with mentored support, Ed changed the climate of leadership. He saw his job and that of his mentor team was not to solve problems, but to teach others to identify the most important issues and find solutions together with their teams. He ensured that sufficient positive reinforcement accompanied the efforts, and when the organizational metrics began to shift in a positive direction, he made sure that the information was transparent and celebrated as short-term wins indicative of progress.

Within months, Ed reached a tipping point of leadership energy. Employees saw the conversations on strategic thinking bring out business environment conditions of which they were less aware and felt drawn to the opportunities for being more successful. The focus on technical credibility greatly improved computer reliability and customer interactions. Employees began to surface new ideas and challenge old assumptions in the new inclusive environment created through the overall development effort. At the five-month milestone, people began seeing positive indicators of improvement and felt a momentum about the new strategic and inclusive atmosphere. By eight months, kudos began coming in from headquarters about the turnaround and at fourteen months, it was clear the performance improvement was sustainable and not simply a quick-fix initiative. Corporate management formally announced that it would retain both computing centers due to increased efficiency.

Ed was then selected for a promotion in headquarters to oversee research and development and his successor at the center was selected from within. What remained the same despite the personnel changeover was the embedded learning behavior that Ed created: think strategically, bolster technical competence, coach and grow leadership capabilities at all levels, and be inclusive in signing up everyone to lead. Three years later, Ed's information technology division continued to be known for spinning off great leaders for elsewhere in the organization and for sustainable breakthrough performance.

A Call to Action

This book is meant to spur a leader's thinking about work at all leadership levels and functions and at the same time guide personal and family accomplishments. My contention is that you can use the strengths, clarity, and focus approach to face any challenge and achieve breakthrough results. My experience as an employee for nearly all of my life, including working on the family farm with my father, and as a manager for the vast majority of my career informs this approach. I also perform extensive research in the leadership field based on statistical analysis of surveys and assessments as a political scientist and leadership and organizational researcher.

From my days as a boy working on my father's farm until today, I can specifically recall times when the strengths, clarity, and focus approach yielded more than average success. My father considered his children as strengths to tackle the tons of farm work that needed to get done. He would provide clarity for the task and ask each of us to focus on our work. When I was ten years old, I started cultivating soybeans with a small tractor with a two-row cultivator while my brother covered four rows with his larger tractor. The strength of this approach was obvious as we could definitely cover more ground in the field while my father would tend to other duties. He continually clarified to us that what he valued most was that we didn't ruin the crop by mistakenly digging up soybean rows from lack of attention. He demanded constant focus on our task and my brother thought that singing while cultivating soybeans would help them grow. While I can't positively say that the singing helped, the focus surely did.

One year, we planted significantly more crops than usual and my father needed to acquire another combine to help with the harvest. We went to a local used farm machinery dealer and selected a combine that my father thought my brother could handle. The problem was that it wasn't in working condition and we had to refurbish it to get it running. For the next month, I watched my father deploy his strengths, my brother and I, to accomplish this task. I was small and could climb into the machine to hold the nuts as my father tightened all the bolts and connections from the outside to ensure the grain would pass through the machine without obstruction. We successfully accomplished this task in a few weeks and were ready for harvest season. I was proud to watch my father and brother harvest the crops with two combines well suited to their strengths while I did my best to keep up with the trucks hauling the grain. The clarity he provided was that we needed to work quickly when the weather was good to ensure that we harvested the grain at the perfect time to store for the winter. The crops had grown well that year because of very favorable weather and the focus was not to let anything go to waste. That year was the best my father had on the farm in years and he used strengths, clarity, and focus to achieve those breakthrough results.

When my brother left for college and it was only my father and I who worked the fields, he knew that we now needed new equipment that would deliver more efficiency. He bought a new combine and a grain dryer so that we wouldn't have to depend on getting the harvest in at just the right time. He could dry the grain if it was a bit damp when harvested in the early morning or late afternoon. I never expected that he would ask me to drive the combine, but I suppose he felt his strength was operating the grain dryer while I harvested the crops. As I entered the field on the first day of harvest, he watched to ensure I was applying the right focus for the task. It wasn't long before I noticed a large rock go into the combine and I reacted immediately to shut down the auger to prevent the rock from actually going into the machine. I stopped the combine and my father appeared in a few seconds to ask what the problem was. As he watched me pull the rock from the front auger of the machine causing no damage, all he said was "good job." Believe me, for my father, that was very high praise indeed and he was quite pleased even though he didn't obviously show it. That year we took shifts combining the grain and drying it during the day and plowing the fields at night and it was amazing when we harvested a field of grain, dried it, and then turned it to a black plowed field overnight and that was another outstanding year for the farm.

At an early age, I decided I wanted to be a pilot and when I asked my high school counselor what was the best way to do that; he replied to go to the Air Force Academy. So I assessed my strengths and clarified my goal to secure a Congressional nomination to attend the academy with a laser focus on becoming a pilot. I can't cite the number of times I had to remember the clarity of purpose I needed to make it through that four-year academy ordeal and I applied the right focus to achieve my goal. I had more challenges in pilot training after graduation, but again I remembered my clear purpose and focused on finishing the program with distinction. I guess I succeeded because I was one of only two new pilots in my class assigned to fighter aircraft upon graduation. I suppose I was a natural for flying fighters as I excelled in my F-4 training and finished at the top of my class. I was assigned to Germany to fly the F-4 and shortly after

I arrived, the base was scheduled to transition to flying the F-16. Again, strengths, clarity, and focus garnered me one of the only two lieutenant slots to fly the new aircraft at the base.

I spent 22 years in the Air Force flying fighters and working staff jobs and I can remember the times when I used the strengths, clarity, and focus approach to achieve great success. I also recall a few setbacks in my career when I didn't apply the approach and I either failed or achieved less than desirable results. We all make mistakes, but I distinctly remember not following the principles that had worked so well for me in the past. I probably got complacent thinking that I would always achieve success just because of who I was. Well, I was mistaken.

When I was ready to retire from the Air Force, I had the choice of continuing to fly with the airlines as a commercial pilot as many of my friends did or continuing to work in the Federal government in civil service with another government agency. I assessed my strengths and I knew that I wouldn't be happy with "flying a bus" and being away from home sixty to seventy percent of the time. I applied to many Federal government positions and finally succeeded with my selection into the Internal Revenue Service's (IRS) Senior Executive Service Candidate Development Program. That program was unique because all candidates who successfully completed the program had a senior executive job waiting for them after graduation. Again, the strengths, clarity, and focus approach was my ally in this endeavor.

Shortly after earning my senior executive position with the IRS, I completed my doctorate degree in political science with an emphasis in international politics. I remember when I chose the political science field as opposed to other choices. I wanted to eventually work as an instructor at the Air Force Academy and they told me that the best chance I had was in the largest departments there...math or political science. Well, I considered my strengths and figured that I was much better as sitting around a coffee table discussing politics than I was at solving complex math problems. Of course, as it turns out, the political science field has more to do with surveys and statistical research than I thought, and I discovered that statistics was actually one of my hidden strengths. And I also discovered that the academic culture wouldn't meet my interests as my goal was always to help students learn and that is far down the list of important issues in the academic world. The ability to bring in grant money for research and writing journal articles always takes precedence over being a good instructor. What a shame!

My first senior executive job in the IRS was interesting because it was when IRS Commissioner Charles Rossotti was transforming the agency to focus on both customer service and tax compliance at the same time. Nearly everyone in the agency had always figured that those two issues were on opposite ends of a pendulum; if you increased one, the other had to decrease. Mr. Rossotti provided the clear expectation that the IRS could do both well and best serve taxpayers while still assuring the highest tax compliance for the country. I led the leadership and organizational effectiveness organization that designed and delivered leadership and organizational development to the agency to support the transformation. My years in the IRS proved particularly successful as the IRS established best practices in leadership and organizational development recognized by many outside evaluators and agencies. As a matter of fact, when the Federal Bureau of Investigation (FBI) faced a transformation from criminal investigation after crimes to seeking intelligence information to stop terrorist crimes before they occurred, they recruited me to lead the prestigious FBI Academy at Quantico, Virginia to arm the workforce with the competence necessary to accomplish that bold mission.

Early accomplishment of a Presidential directive on focused intelligence training, learning simulations involving teams of intelligence officers and special agents, and a new focus on leadership development marked my time in the FBI. I applied my strengths, clarity, and focus approach to great success and yet, a few in the law enforcement world had a hard time seeing the strength of a professional learning executive's approach against the experience of all previous heads of the FBI Academy who wore badges and carried weapons. I even mounted one of the six barrels from an F-16 Gatling gun on a plaque in my office and many thought it was an air refueling probe because of its size. Even when I explained that was only one barrel of my weapon, it did little to change the culture. I highly respect law enforcement professionals, but sometimes the culture impedes progress.

Subsequently, the Federal Aviation Administration (FAA) needed someone to oversee the hiring and training of 17,000 air traffic controllers in the next five years. After President Ronald Reagan fired striking controllers in 1981, the FAA hired thousands of replacements all at once and now all those controllers were approaching retirement after 25 years of service.

The FAA indentified strengths in me to successfully accomplish this role as they had watched my career progress. When I arrived, FAA senior officials clarified expectations of me by demanding that I get them off the front page of the Washington Post for the lack of preparedness to hire and train so many air traffic controllers so quickly! As I undertook that task, I discovered that the organizations involved in hiring and training air traffic controllers all had separate organizational performance measures and they could claim success on their piece of the task even though the overall task wasn't getting done! Actually, that probably describes a typical government agency more focused on activity than outcomes. So, I needed to apply my strengths to clarify a new expectation that everyone now was responsible for achieving the overall outcome of hiring the right number of air traffic controllers in the right places. I partnered with the Finance Office to create a Controller Workforce Plan to determine the correct number of controllers needed to manage the commercial air traffic demand…the first of its kind!

We established monthly controller on board figures to gauge our effectiveness and while we had to change hiring and training processes on the fly, we finally achieved the end-of-year controller on board number during my first year there and got the FAA off the front page of the Washington Post! The strength of a common clear goal and focus on the right processes to achieve that shared goal made a huge difference. Those processes eventually drove the controller hiring and training program to new heights that even the Inspector General had to appreciate: "The FAA has done what anyone would consider as an admirable job of hiring and training air traffic controllers." While it was truly a team effort, the FAA gave me the prestigious **Air Traffic Organization Leadership Award** that year for the effort.

Again, we didn't resolve all issues, and most of those missteps were cases where we didn't stringently follow the strengths, clarity, and focus approach. In spite of these setbacks, when the President's Management Council (PMC), consisting of the Deputy Secretaries of the 20 largest Federal government agencies, looked for someone to lead a government-wide senior executive development initiative to face challenges of smaller budgets, growing mission demands, and increased complexity, they contacted and hired me. The PMC wanted to bring senior executives from all across government to reach new levels of creative thinking and collaboration to deliver the highest levels of government performance and results. The PMC had clear expectations of me to deliver an unprecedented coordination and collaboration effort called *Leading EDGE* (Executives Driving Government Excellence) comprised of five integrated learning components (workshops, Government Performance Projects (GPPs), assessments, executive coaching, and a sophisticated web portal) in just four months! Believe me, focusing the efforts of over a hundred Federal government agencies on designing and delivering the best program possible was daunting. And yet again, the strengths, clarity, and focus approach delivered again on a program that over 90 percent of senior executives felt was highly relevant to their job and would recommend to a colleague, with an unprecedented savings from executive team Government Performance Projects saving over $1.4 billion the first year!

In my current role as the Chief Learning Officer of the Office of Information and Technology within the Department of Veterans Affairs, I am the primary advocate to embed organizational learning as a key business strategy for mission accomplishment by boosting workforce competence in technical, professional, and functional fields to meet the growing needs of Veterans. Employing the strengths, clarity, and focus approach has led the office to deliver tremendous value across all aspects of employee, leadership, and organizational development exhibited by an unprecedented increase in workforce competence to accomplish the mission from 61 to 71 percent. Satisfaction with training skyrocketed 13 percent with notable skill gap closures of 13 percent in human factors engineering, 10 percent in risk management, and 5 percent in enterprise network defense, information assurance, and organizational awareness. The Chief Learning Office earned the Association for Talent Development's (ATD) prestigious **Excellence in Practice Award** for the effort. Our collaboration effort with the Office of Information Security to design a two-year onboarding program for Information Security Officers received the **Government Information Security Leadership Award (GISLA)**.

Book's Journey

I'm not telling you all of this to impress you with my personal accomplishments, but to sell the adoption of a simple, yet effective way of accomplishing work and achieving breakthrough results. To make this point in the second chapter, I encourage you to think differently— yes, totally differently—about many of the ways you have approached problem solving in the past and realize that we live in a remedial world of primarily analyzing what's wrong. The third chapter focuses on leveraging strengths to achieve breakthrough performance results and provides some examples to drive that point home. The fourth chapter highlights the value of providing clarity to your workforce, project teammates, family, etc. to define what success looks like. I then take a detour in the fifth chapter to discuss my important research on the "vital few" accelerators of leadership effectiveness, employee engagement, and workforce productivity. The sixth chapter highlights the significance of focus as the most important competency of the 21st century. The seventh chapter summarizes the approach and discusses the business case for adopting the strengths, clarity, and focus approach. And finally, chapter eight includes a checklist to apply the strengths, clarity, and focus approach to any challenge to achieve breakthrough performance improvements.

CHAPTER 2

THINKING DIFFERENTLY

Our world is not shaped by those who think similarly, but by those who dare to think differently.

—Rashida Rowe

Throughout history, people with new ideas, who think differently and try to change things, have always been called troublemakers.

—Richelle Mead

The problem is that we humans are deep conformists.

—Robert Greene

It is hard to think differently. To change your world, change your thoughts.

—Debasish Mridha

Leadership and learning are indispensable to each other.

—John Fitzgerald Kennedy

When discussing the strengths, clarity, and focus approach with various audiences, I first ask them about the proudest moments they have had at work and what aspect of work most motivates them. The answers I hear usually revolve around personal or staff successes, significant organizational accomplishments, or the importance of the organization's mission. This reminds me of the results of a recent Merit Systems Protection Board (MSPB) survey of Federal employees that revealed that 98 percent of these workers were motivated by pride in their work (Rutzick, 2006). Now that's a significant percentage and nearly an absolute! Government employees, and probably the vast majority of employees in many other professions, define success and generate motivation from pride in their work. This is an important concept that we will return to and derive some significant leadership lessons from a bit later.

The Power of Thinking Differently

To start this discussion, I truly believe that we need to think differently to apply the strengths, clarity, and focus approach to leadership and I dare say…all situations. And I don't mean that we should simply be thinking "outside-the-box" as that isn't enough to encompass my belief that we really do need to think differently. I also believe that thinking differently is extremely difficult perhaps because of the way that we've been taught to approach difficult situations. My contention is that we tend to think alike… especially when it relates to approaching work or challenging situations, often referred to as "wicked problems." I know that many of you are thinking: "What are you talking about, Jim? We all have different experiences, different heritages, different personalities, different perceptions, and different outlooks on life in general. We already think differently by nature." Well, perhaps that doesn't tell the whole story, so let's explore this a little more and find out.

How many of us are extremely busy at work? How many of us have been asked to do more with less? And how many of us have been asked to do more with less for quite some time now? I'd venture to say that nearly all of you have experienced these realities. My reality is similar and I now believe that I've been asked to do more with less for so long that my only choice is to do less! However, the less that I do must have more impact. Now if I could only figure out which of the many things I do has the most impact, right?

Problem Solving

How many of us have distinguished ourselves at work and/or have been identified by our colleagues and supervisors as problem solvers? When I ask this question to the many audiences that I speak to, I normally see at least 80 percent of the group raise their hands. So, for all of us proud problem solvers, let's talk about a typical day in the life of a problem solver. What do proud problem solvers look for when they arrive at work every morning? I guess we look for problems and usually don't have any trouble finding some or if we can't find any, perhaps we create some to become more useful. And when problem solvers find a problem, I suppose we fix them, right? Isn't that the sequence or am I leaving out some important steps between finding a problem and fixing it?

I guess the first step in the problem solving sequence is to analyze the situation, right? So, in this case, what do proud problem solvers choose to study? We can either study what's wrong or study what's right. It seems logical that we would want to start by analyzing what's wrong. In other words, if there's a problem out there, we need to find out specifically what's wrong in order to fix it, right? I suppose we figure that if we analyze the problem and find out what we are doing wrong, we will just stop doing that and achieve success because the opposite of failure is success, right?

So, now that we've analyzed what's wrong, we need to apply some management principles in order to fix it. Over the years, we have learned many different techniques to apply in these situations. Some of us are old enough to remember the Total Quality Management (TQM) approach and I suspect that many are still using that technique today. TQM became somewhat overshadowed by International Organization for Standardization or ISO 9000 and a few other ISO numbers. Then we seemed to migrate to Business Process Reengineering as a promising new technique of solving problems. I may not have the correct timeline here, but I think Six Sigma came next in the ongoing mantra of problem-solving approaches. Then came Lean and then perhaps because of an ongoing health trend, along came Lean Six Sigma! In the IT world, Great Britain has established the Information Technology Infrastructure Library or ITIL standards to guide successful IT customer service. I probably shouldn't neglect the mention of systems thinking as well. There are probably some newer problem-solving approaches out there as well, but I'm not schooled in the latest process improvement techniques.

Problem-Solving Examples

Perhaps it might help to approach the problem-solving discussion by relating some stories. I once heard a story about some psychology researchers many years ago who endeavored to find the secret to a successful marriage. They wanted to conduct some scholarly research, discover the secret, and then publish their conclusion in an academic or professional journal. So, they discussed how they would undertake the research. Would they study successful or unsuccessful marriages? Initially, they chose to study unsuccessful marriages because after all, that was the problem, right? So, they gathered evidence from 150 unsuccessful marriages and discovered that in the vast majority of these relationships, the spouses argued a lot! They scratched their heads and figured they couldn't get a scholarly journal to publish an article saying that the secret to a successful marriage is to not argue! So, at that point, they decided to also study 150 successful marriages and discovered that in most of those relationships, the spouses argued a lot as well! Finally, they figured that the secret to a successful marriage resided in the space between arguments... hallelujah! The researchers then set out to find what was right in the time space between arguments in the successful marriages. They concluded that the secret to a successful marriage is for one spouse to find the best possible explanation for the other spouse's behavior...and believe it! I'm not sure that qualifies as scholarly research, but my point is that they initially chose to study what was wrong instead of what was right.

Many organizations seek help from consultants when a problem exists. Of course, in most cases, organizational problems usually occur as a result of bad leadership. Thus, to solve a leadership problem, a choice exists to study what's wrong...the bad leaders, or what's right...the good leaders. And, unfortunately, most often we choose to study what's wrong. We discover all the behaviors of the bad leaders and then pronounce to the organization that if leaders would stop the bad behavior, the organization will succeed because the opposite of failure is success. I've heard Marcus Buckingham ask this question of his audiences: "What do you get when you tell a bad manager what not to do?" His answer: "You get a manager who's not bad!" Does that mean that leadership will now start exhibiting great behavior to drive organizational success? How could that occur if we never analyzed what that great behavior is?

Let me illustrate another example regarding our almost instinctive inclination to solve a problem by studying what's wrong rather than discovering what's working well. If a speaker was delivering a presentation to an audience, but was constantly flipping a pen up and catching it on the way down during the talk, the audience would most likely notice the pen flipping more than the quality of the presentation. But, what if the speaker suddenly stopped flipping the pen? Would we now praise the speaker's presentation unquestioningly or just note that he/she was no longer annoying us? In other words, if we eliminated the failing speaker's flipping pen problem, would that alone constitute a successful presentation? It's obvious that we can't achieve success by just studying failure and then no longer performing the failing actions.

I see that logic applied to myriad situations as if it's our default action to analyze a problem by focusing on what's wrong. We live in a remedial world. The world is a problem to solve. To learn more about health, we study disease more than we analyze wellness. To learn more about weather, we study storms more than we analyze a sunny day. To learn about mental health, we study depression more than we analyze joy. To learn about our environment, we study pollutants more than we analyze clean air. And the list goes on and on. Thus, the contention I raised at the start of this discussion that we all tend to think similarly about problem solving and few of us really think differently to discover how to leverage success rather than correct weaknesses seems more plausible.

An Alternative

But focusing on analyzing what's wrong isn't incorrect. Many of us problem solvers have achieved some improvement by following the common path to analyze what's wrong and correct weaknesses. However, in my experience, the improvements gained were mostly incremental and while we were pleased, those small improvements only caused our supervisors to ask for more. So, we had to repeat the process again and again to make us even busier and achieve more incremental improvements! The alternative I offer is that by studying what's right with any situation and leveraging success, the possibility for breakthrough performance opens up that delivers many more results with the same level of effort. I offer Figure 1 to illustrate my point (Trinka, 2005). With the same level of effort, leveraging success clearly delivers more results than merely a traditional problem-solving approach of correcting weaknesses.

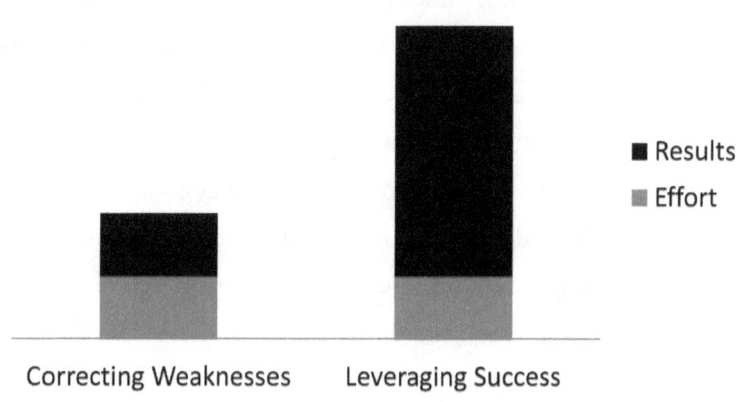

Figure 1: Problem-Solving Approach Comparison

At the beginning of this discussion, I asked what at work makes you proud and motivates you to perform. I could have asked about what disappoints you or what challenges you face at work. Would that have felt differently? Usually when I ask about negative experiences, it seems as though someone has let the air out of the room. Everyone remembers and focuses on that negativity and that's hard for anyone to overcome. Analyzing success and what's right simply feels better psychologically than focusing on failure and weaknesses (Achor, 2010). You might have also noticed that I didn't put any numbers on the chart I just showed you. Of course I didn't! Otherwise, you're likely to hold me accountable for any specific numbers I cite! So, for now, let's suspend judgment on my contention that a focus on leveraging success delivers breakthrough results while resolving problems by correcting weaknesses simply leads to incremental performance improvement.

Chances are that the first questions you were taught to ask when you became a manager went something like this. What's not working? What are your challenges? What are our weaknesses? Even if you were taught to use a full spectrum set of questions like those in a SWOT (Strengths, Weaknesses, Opportunities, Threats) analysis, most likely you zeroed right in on the problems and weaknesses. This is not evil nor is it bad advice.

However, I'm proposing that leaders would benefit from looking more closely at what works and finding ways to do more or leverage that success even more. This is not about an either/or choice of focusing on problems or successes. It is about ensuring leaders are as focused on appreciating what's working well and helping the organization learn from those successes as they are on finding what's not working. The premise is that an organization that keeps focusing on problems will find more and more things that don't work well. An organization looking to discover what works best will continue to find more and more that is good. Leaders use appreciative inquiry as a process for engaging people across the organization around what works (Cooperrider, 1999). The positive psychological effects of looking for and finding success will further engage a workforce to achieve success and improve perceptions of your leadership effectiveness at the same time (Achor, 2010).

I'm not suggesting that you abandon the correcting weaknesses approach. I merely suggest that you may benefit more by first asking "What's working well?" or "What are our greatest successes?" This approach makes traditional managers and leaders nervous. We are so ingrained to study the problem that it feels disingenuous to start the other way around. It's not either/or!

Perhaps thinking differently to capitalize more on analyzing what's right and then leveraging that success provides the opportunity to do less, but yet have more impact. I remember seeing a book title a few years ago written by Marcus Buckingham that read: *The One Thing You Need to Know…About Great Managing, Great Leading, and Sustained Individual Success* (2005). I was so excited to buy that book that it literally jumped off the bookshelf into my hands. The idea that someone could tell me to do fewer things…or only one thing…to achieve individual and leadership success greatly intrigued me and has guided my research for years. I have a simple mind and I need to approach any situation with the least complexity as possible. So why not develop a much shorter To-Do list knowing that by doing these few things well, you will have great impact?

Figure 2 summarizes the disparity of the thinking alike and thinking differently perspectives:

	Thinking Alike	Thinking Differently
Perspective	Problem solvers correct weaknesses	Problem solvers leverage success
	View the world as remedial and study failure to illuminate success	View the world optimistically and look for ways to build on previous successes
Consequences	Sustain negative energy and lack of engagement	Build positive energy, engagement, and momentum

Figure 2: Thinking Alike vs. Thinking Differently

CHAPTER 3

LEVERAGING STRENGTHS

Our fulfillment in life and career meets with success when we give our best as per our unique talent, gifting, strengths while willing to team up with others in the areas of our limitations.

—Assegid Habtewold

The best organization and managers gather their strengths together and make their weaknesses irrelevant.

—Peter Drucker

The best way to bring this work alive is to become aware on a daily basis of your unique package of strengths and how it best serves you and the world at large.

—Laurie Rosenfeld

Success is achieved by developing our strengths, not by eliminating our weaknesses.

—Marilyn vas Savant

A leader needs to know his strengths as a carpenter knows his tools, or as a physician knows the instruments at her disposal. What great leaders have in common is that each truly knows his or her strengths – and can call on the right strength at the right times.

—Don Clifton

T he first item on the very short manager's To-Do list I'm presenting to you deals with leveraging strengths to achieve breakthrough performance results.

The Best Leader You've Worked For or With

Now, let me ask you to think about the *best* leader that you've ever worked for or with. I know some of you might be thinking of yourselves, but please think of someone else. When you think of that *best* leader, what were some of the strengths of that person? In other words, exactly what were the behaviors, characteristics, or competencies that made the *best* leader you ever worked for or with stand out above all others? When I ask this of the many audiences I speak to, I invariably get only a small number of very similar responses. I hear things like empowering, fair, good communicator, trusting, honest, and open. I can usually group the responses into only six to eight categories. And I often hear a story about that *best* leader assigning work to you that was a bit daunting, but he/she provided encouragement, empowerment, and the support necessary for you to not only succeed, but also excel at the work, which resulted in tremendous growth and development for you. When a manager has great confidence in you, sets high standards for you, and challenges you to achieve goals that you never thought you could grasp on your own, that behavior produces lasting impact and you consider that leader the *best* you ever worked for or with. And, interestingly, I hear the same comments no matter what audience I speak to in different professions, different countries, different generations, etc. It seems that we all describe great leadership in similar ways.

And then I ask the audience if the *best* leaders they were thinking of had any weaknesses? Almost unanimously, they say yes. Say it isn't so! The *best* leaders you ever worked for or with had weaknesses? My follow-on question is: "Why didn't those weaknesses matter to you?" Eventually, someone answers with the phrase: "His/her strengths outweighed the weaknesses." Fascinating! So, let's review. I just conducted a very unscientific study of leadership. And did I attempt to study what's wrong… the bad leaders or what's right…the good leaders? Not only did I try to analyze what's right…the good leaders, but those who the audience actually considered the *best* leaders they ever worked for or with. And I discovered that the *best* leaders have only a small number of strengths consistent across various populations *and* had some weaknesses, but the strengths outweighed the weaknesses! It seems that we don't identify our *best* leaders by an absence of shortcomings, but rather by the attributes that lead to their success and what does work. My question then simply is: "Why have instructors, coaches, consultants, and organizations in general tried to improve leadership by correcting weaknesses for decades when we consider strengths more importantly than weaknesses?" I realize that strengths-based development has grown in recent years, but still the vast majority of leadership development concentrates on identifying and correcting weaknesses to improve behavior. As problem solvers, we apparently see leadership as something we think we can fix!

A Strength-Based Approach Example

I want to relate a story that illustrates the effectiveness of the strength-based approach to leadership development. When I was in the IRS, we administered 360-degree assessments to every manager who took a leadership development course. I decided to personally lead the interpretation sessions for the managers who just took those assessments. I still hadn't accepted the strength-based approach and even though I thought that I had done a great job of interpreting the results of the 360-degree assessments and guiding participants on a sound development path of correcting weaknesses, I observed that the evaluations for those sessions were still quite low. When I thought more about it, I realized that something was inherently wrong with the "correcting weaknesses" approach. The traditional method of focusing on correcting weaknesses was at best, producing only incremental improvement. After all, we were asking managers to improve on activities that they knew they weren't particularly good at, didn't enjoy performing (perhaps disliked doing), and that others just confirmed they didn't score very well in those competencies! That didn't sound like a particularly successful prescription for improvement, yet that's exactly the guidance we provided our managers. We even tried to mask this practice by using language such as focusing on "challenges" or "developmental opportunities," but it was transparent that we were attempting to correct a leader's weaknesses and that approach, subtle or not, conveyed distinctly negative connotations. What was worse was that we displayed leaders' 360-degree assessment results against "average" scores for each competency, which unknowingly perpetuated leadership mediocrity. If the managers scored just "above average" (a C grade), they had little motivation to improve. In many ways, good had become the enemy of excellent and we needed to challenge ourselves to develop our leaders into something more than just average.

I then decided to analyze the 360-degree assessments of thousands of IRS managers (Trinka, 2004). A daunting task for sure, but that revealed some very interesting results on the competencies that differentiated "great" leaders in the top ten percent from the rest. That's right; I chose to evaluate the highest scoring or "great" leaders to discover what differentiated them from the rest. Of the twenty-one leadership competencies in the IRS model, only eleven competencies differentiated great leaders in the top ten percent from the rest (see Figure 3 on next page). Furthermore, IRS leaders needed to display profound strengths (scores in the top ten percent of their peers on that item) in only four of these eleven competencies for others to perceive them as a "great" leader in the top ten percent. The research results also provided fascinating empirical evidence to confirm the value of diversity in IRS leaders, as strengths in any four of the eleven key competencies engendered perceptions of "great" leadership.

Core Management Areas				
Leadership	**Employee Engagement**	**Customer Focus**	**Achieving Results**	**Building Relationships**
Communication	Develops Others	External Awareness	Achieves Goals	Collaboration
Critical, Strategic Thinking	Influencing/ Negotiating	Partnering	Political Savvy	Leverages Diversity
			Technical Credibility	

Figure 3: Key "Differentiating" Competencies

Interestingly, these key differentiating competencies typically balance across core management areas such as leadership, employee engagement, customer focus, achieving results, and building relationships. You might notice that a few common competencies are missing from the key differentiating competency list—for example—integrity and honesty. I'm certainly not implying that concepts like integrity, honesty, and teamwork (also absent) are not important, since they are crucial competencies for all leaders to possess. These areas do not "differentiate" great leaders from the rest because the vast majority of managers score very highly in these competencies on 360-degree assessments. And since it is often better to be distinct rather than extinct, the implication is that you are better off focusing on the differentiators for development.

The concept of key differentiating competencies implies that leaders can now focus developmental resources on improving a shorter list of competencies instead of diffusing training efforts on an organization's entire list of leadership competencies. Most managers remark that they don't have time to focus on development anyway and besides, they are aware that previous efforts have not proved particularly effective. Instead of lengthening an already time-pressed manager's "to-do" list, this study offered a method of focusing that list to include only those items that were likely to have the greatest impact on improving leadership effectiveness and business results.

This study confirmed that one doesn't need to be a superhero to be a "great" leader. As we learned earlier, most people cite only three to four profound strengths when they think of the *best* leader that they have worked for or with. In fact, when asked whether that same leader also exhibited some weaknesses, most said "yes" and were quick to point out that those weaknesses didn't matter because the strengths were so profound. In effect, the presence of a few profound strengths created a "halo effect" that overshadowed perceptions of weaknesses. Thus, we must fully consider the power of perception when developing our leaders.

As a result of this study, I then encouraged IRS leaders in their 360-degree assessment interpretation sessions to build at least one more of the key differentiating competencies that others already identified as a strong area (80th percentile) to an even higher level above the 90th percentile. This innovative method attempted to take advantage of the power of perception and created that "halo effect" for a manager where others valued strengths so much that they overshadowed any weaknesses. Rather than feeling pressure and guilt about correcting weaknesses, these IRS leaders experienced the positive energy generated by an identification and further development of strengths, which generated considerable motivation for behavioral change. Using the findings gleaned from this study, IRS leaders achieved over 60 percent improvement in individual leadership effectiveness measured by 360-degree assessments! Good does not equal "great," and all organizations need more great leaders.

My research also uncovered that five of the key competencies (Communication; Develops Others; Critical, Strategic Thinking; Achieves Goals; and Collaboration) develop all of the other eleven differentiating competencies as well. This finding implied that we could refocus a dauntingly long list of competencies to a much shorter list of key characteristics that our great leaders possessed and then develop just five of those to have the greatest development impact on all of the differentiators. We now made the problem much more manageable from an individual leader's perspective and could make good leaders "great" without lengthening their "To-Do" list. Leaders clearly improved their effectiveness much more than the traditional approach and thankfully, my 360-assessment interpretation sessions generated much higher levels of satisfaction.

The Essence of Great Leadership

I sometimes get asked by organizations to come in and help them with a problem they are experiencing. Since most organizational problems are leadership related, one of the first actions that I take is to stop employees in the hallways and ask them the question: "How would you describe "great" leadership in this organization?" From those employees who don't run away from me, most often I get the answer: "I know great leadership when I see it." Of course, being a researcher, that answer doesn't have enough detail for me, so I ask more probing questions. More often than not, those questions result in employees expressing this sentiment: "The best leader considers my success equal to or more important than their own success...and I know it when I see it!" That revelation certainly makes things simpler for leaders to achieve greatness...at least in the eyes of their employees. Just treat your employees' success equal to or more importantly than your own success and you as a leader, and thus the organization itself, will succeed. And the thing is...leaders can't fake that behavior because employees "know it when they see it." Seems simple, but for some of us, it might be a difficult proposition.

In summary then, I follow a strength-based approach to every situation I encounter since I probably not only learned that from my father, but also discovered this secret through many trials and errors in my work and home life. I'm not saying that the correcting weaknesses approach is wrong, just merely that the strength-based approach has a much higher chance of achieving breakthrough results, thus allowing us to do more by focusing on less. It certainly worked for Ed in my example in chapter 1. Figure 4 on the next page summarizes the difference between the correcting weaknesses and leveraging strengths approaches:

	Correcting Weaknesses	**Leveraging Strengths**
Focus of Analysis	What isn't working	What is working
Actions	Stop doing what isn't working to achieve success—the opposite of failure is success	Find ways of doing more of what's working to leverage and accelerate success
Results	Incremental Improvement	Breakthrough Improvement

Figure 4: Correcting Weaknesses vs. Leveraging Strengths

CHAPTER 4

PROVIDING CLARITY

We, your followers, are anxious about the future. To turn our anxiety into confidence, you must tell us why we will win. You must tell us why we will prevail in this better future you seem to see so clearly.

—Marcus Buckingham

The future we predict today is not inevitable. We can influence it, if we know what we want it to be.

—Charles Handy

The future is not some place we are going to, but a place we are creating.

—John Schaar

When your goals are clear, you will come up with exactly the right answer at exactly the right time.

—Brian Tracy

The second item on the very short manager's To-Do list I'm presenting to you deals with providing clarity to reduce uncertainty. To begin the discussion on this important issue, I'm again going to use a few stories to illustrate how important this concept is in both work and home environments. One thing that everyone will probably agree with me on is that we, as humans, don't have very many things in common. However, I contend that one of the very few things we do have in common is that none of us know what will happen to us in the future with any certainty. I was in New Orleans a short time ago and, while I was walking on Bourbon Street, I was given a flyer that declared that Natasha could foretell my future for a modest investment of $20. Certainly, some people seem to have a knack for correctly predicting a few future events, but the likelihood of those individuals trying to scam us in predicting our future is incredibly high.

Driving Into the Fog

What do we do when we suddenly drive into fog on the road? When I ask that question to the audiences I speak to, many answers emerge such as turning on lights to better see (or perhaps for others to better see us), paying more attention to road lines and other markings for guidance, and of course slowing down! So, it seems like a natural reaction to proceeding into the unknown is to slow down. Does that have any parallels to the work environment? I think you'll agree that it most certainly means that when an organization faces uncertainty, the natural reaction of its employees and perhaps most leaders, is to slow down or question the decision to keep charging ahead at full speed as some leaders call for.

Have you ever been with a group wanting to go out for dinner to a nice restaurant? How was the decision made on which restaurant to go to or, for that matter, which type of food the group would prefer? Has a group ever assigned you to make the excruciating decision on which restaurant or type of food would be best? When that happens, we think of the many ways to arrive at such a decision and remember that we live in a democracy, so perhaps we have people vote on a particular location. That usually doesn't work since we might disappoint the minority into not even attending the dinner altogether. Or perhaps you make a list and have people mark their preferences on the list. Again, this usually doesn't produce the best outcome. But, have you ever noticed that in the midst of this difficult decision-making process, someone just suggests a place? Let's say, in this case, someone suggests an Italian restaurant. Quite often, as most are frustrated with other decision-making methods, people start agreeing with the suggestion. All of a sudden, this choice seems very plausible and you thankfully toss away your decision-making matrix!

As the day passes and dinner time approaches, you notice that you are now looking forward to the meal and you notice others are commenting on what they might order from the menu. You overhear someone speaking of lasagna, others of spaghetti and meatballs, a few about chicken parmesan, and even the occasion mention of chicken alfredo or linguini ai frutti di mare. People seem to actually look forward to the occasion and usually for a reason you can't begin to imagine. Let's look at this more closely. Attending a group dinner had everyone feeling a little uneasy about the event and someone provided clarity by suggesting a place to go. Someone provided clarity on the future and it positively changed the conversation. While this seems like a simple and generally common occurrence, it has great implications in both the family and work environments. To maintain a constant speed and positive outlook on the future, a leader needs to provide clarity to their people to reduce the uncertainty of the future. That's an incredibly important discovery and we again find that we can learn important lessons as we tackle the most common of occurrences.

Organizational Clarity

As it turns out, successful businesses know this simple fact. Corporations that succeed find that clarity and make it clear to their employees. For example, most agree that Microsoft is a successful corporation, yet do we know what makes them a success? Certainly, Microsoft is famous for software, yet many would disagree on the effectiveness or user-friendly nature of its software. We all remember the early personal computer days of hitting save often to prevent the loss of a significant amount of work. And who can forget the "blue screen" of death when your computer monitor suddenly turned blue when a fatal error occurred and all your work was lost? As it turns out, software alone isn't what makes Microsoft a successful company. In reality, Microsoft's strength is actually in making the best deals with other players in the computing business. Have you noticed that in most cases, when you purchase a personal computer, it already comes loaded with Microsoft software? That didn't come about by accident or coincidence. Microsoft makes great deals! When I was in the IRS senior executive development program, we visited the Microsoft headquarters and listened as we heard the CEO tell us how he greets every new employee during orientation and passes along the secret to Microsoft's success and encourages anyone who comes up with an idea for a great deal to get the word to him directly as that's Microsoft's competitive advantage.

Another example: The Apple corporation literally changed the world with some of it products. Apple has the uncanny knack of building a "rabidly loyal" customer base. Have you ever tried to convince a Macintosh user to change to a PC? As you know, that effort will most likely fail and, as a matter of course, the Mac user will likely become visibly annoyed with you! How does Apple build that loyal of a customer base? Quite simply, Apple has an uncanny ability to innovate handy and user-friendly conveniences before customers even know they need them. Did you ever imagine a very small digital device that would allow you to listen to all your favorite music anywhere with sound quality rarely delivered by an inexpensive music player? Did you ever imagine a phone that could do many of the things that previously only a large and definitely not portable computer or camera could perform? Apple consistently manages to create small, relatively inexpensive, user-friendly digital devices that make its customers lives easier. That's its competitive advantage. And Apple's leaders provide that clarity to their employees to reduce the uncertainty of the future.

The implications of this concept are huge! Imagine if you could provide that kind of clarity to reduce the uncertainty of the future for your employees, or even for your own family? I've worked in organizations that did, perhaps unknowingly, provided that clarity and then for others that didn't figure out the one thing that drove the organization's success. For example, when I was in the IRS, it was the clarity of mission among employees that obviated the acrimony everyone thinks of when the IRS is mentioned. Most everyone dislikes the IRS, and politicians of both political parties bash the IRS as a form of sport. That has led IRS employees to hunker down and turn inwards for support. Some IRS employees, when asked where they work, avoid the acrimony by saying they work in the Department of Treasury. While it's certainly true that the IRS is a subordinate organization in the Department of Treasury, the employee was quite simply avoiding either disparaging looks or a difficult conversation if he/she would admit to working for the IRS. As a matter of fact, the insular culture at the IRS encouraged employees to find a deeper satisfaction and purpose for their work. The idea of "We Fund America" was alive and frequently discussed among employees. Over 99 percent of the funds that find their way into America's coffers pass through either an IRS employee's hands or through an IRS computer system. IRS employees made the "We Fund America" rallying cry a reality as a motivation and source of pride in their work. However, that concept never made it to a vision or mission statement crafted by senior leadership in the IRS. Frankly, I always thought IRS leaders missed an important opportunity there.

Unfortunately, I didn't notice a similar point of clarity in the next two organizations that I worked in…the FBI or FAA for that matter. The FBI certainly is a very successful law enforcement organization, yet its strength is the proclivity of the agents in the field to succeed in nearly all situations, in some cases, in spite of senior leadership in headquarters attempting to interfere in investigations they know little about. My opinion is that the FBI succeeded in its work based on the reputation and the mystique of being an FBI agent. Many law enforcement professionals aspire to become an FBI agent one day. When the FBI offers its help to state and local law enforcement organizations, it brings many resources, technology, and equipment to supplement the reach of these smaller agencies. My conclusion is thank goodness for the FBI for all it does to keep America safe from terrorism now and perhaps more clarity provided to employees would make the organization even more successful.

Of course, the FAA exists to make flying safe for the American public. Its many departments work on different aspects of that safety and the organization has certainly made flying much safer over the years. However, I could never glean a single rallying cry that provided clarity for FAA employees. I certainly looked for it, and maybe I missed it, and the organization faces constant scrutiny from Congress with the ever-present threat to privatize the operation entirely. Interestingly, the organization uses private sector titles for some of its government senior executive positions like Chief Operating Officer, Senior Vice President, Vice President, and other similar designations. Perhaps the FAA is trying to confuse people into believing it's already privatized! I'm sure that won't work in the case of Congress or the White House for that matter. The FAA typically resides near the bottom of government employee engagement surveys and also the "Best Place to Work in Government" listings (Partnership for Public Service, 2016). Perhaps establishing some clarity in the direction of the agency or its mission might improve that standing by reducing the uncertainty of the future.

I then moved to the Department of Veterans Affairs (VA) and in my second year there, the agency was embroiled in a significant controversy, perhaps scandal, when the Inspector General discovered that some VA medical centers, notably Phoenix and elsewhere, had "cooked" the books when recording the time it took to schedule Veterans for medical appointments. Eventually, the VA Secretary resigned in the face of considerable Congressional scrutiny and unfavorable media reports. A new VA Secretary, Bob McDonald, was nominated and gained Senate confirmation and immediately went about a significant transformation effort. After some significant analysis of what was working in the VA, Secretary McDonald provided this clarity for VA employees. The organization was now all about "Improving the Veteran Experience." That became the rallying cry and the mantra behind all transformation efforts. Since that concept was now the raison d'être of VA's existence, the first new organization he created within VA was the Veteran Experience Office. It certainly made sense that if the organization now existed to improve the Veteran experience, it needed an office designated to discover exactly what that meant.

The Veteran Experience Office subsequently created an innovative Veteran survey with only four questions that rated effectiveness, ease, emotion, and ultimately trust of the Veteran in VA services. So, after a Veteran interacted with VA, he/she was asked to rate the effectiveness and ease of the encounter; how he/she felt about the interaction (emotion or satisfaction); and finally, did he/she trust the VA to perform its mission. Initial scores for this survey ranged in the 40-50 percent range for positive reactions (the combination of agree and strongly agree ratings on a five-point Likert scale) and the VA discovered it had a long way to go to improve the Veteran experience. However, in just twelve months, ratings improved to a range between 60-70 percent positive in all four areas (U.S. Department of Veteran Affairs, 2017). While the VA has a long way to go to achieve its goals on this survey, that's a remarkable increase in a relatively short amount of time!

All around the VA, positive things are happening. In a 2016 Rand study rating all U.S. hospitals and medical centers on 47 different measures of patient satisfaction, the VA rated number one in 45 of the 47 metrics and it tied for first in the other two (Rand Corporation, 2016). The VA mail order pharmacy achieved the number one ranking in the US for the fifth year in a row in 2016. The National Cemetery Administration attained the University of Michigan's American Customer Satisfaction Index (ASCI) highest customer satisfaction rating (96 percent) of all other U.S. organizations in 2016…for the sixth year in a row (ACSI, 2016). By the end of 2016, over 90 percent of VA medical centers achieved same-day service for Veteran inquiries, even though over 4 million more appointments occurred in 2016 than the year prior. While the VA still has a long way to go to gain the trust of Veterans, Congress, and the American people in performing its mission, it has made significant progress.

When the incoming President Donald Trump's administration looked at what the VA was now doing, it retained an appointee from the previous administration's leadership to continue the transformation efforts. Secretary David Shulkin received a unanimous confirmation vote from all one hundred Senators! And the success continues. In 2017, the Journal of the American Medical Association published a study ranking the quality of health care at VA medical centers higher than most local community hospitals (JAMA, 2017). Certainly, the workforce gains powerful clarity when senior leadership clearly articulates the one thing the organization exists to do.

Providing Clarity for Your Organization

So, how can you provide that kind of clarity of the future for your organization and what impact would that have on your employees? What is the one thing that everyone can look to as a rallying cry and a reason for the organization's very existence? I don't know the answer for your particular organization, but certainly that's the question you should ask your employees and leadership. The Gallup organization, primarily under the direction of Marcus Buckingham and Curt Coffman (1999), performed extensive research to discover the employee survey questions that could best measure a new concept called employee engagement. Engagement meant more than just satisfaction for employees. It went beyond to indicate the extent of the employee commitment to someone or something in the organization that made them work harder, deliver more results for the company, and remain with the organization. Gallup came up with only twelve questions that best indicated employee engagement and the first question was: "I know what is expected of me at work." It seems that a manager clarifying expectations for their employees clearly has a positive impact on engagement.

As a summary of the value of providing clarity to an organization's workforce, I'll contrast it with the concept of a leader who doesn't provide the kind of clarity that reduces uncertainty of the future. That's the type of leader who demands compliance and hires and employs people who should "know what they need to do" to make the organization successful. Figure 5 on the next page compares that perspective to the positive consequences of providing clarity to the organization's workforce. Clarity reduces uncertainty; less uncertainty means more commitment; more commitment results in more engagement; more engagement means better business results! The best leaders provide that clarity!

	Promoting Compliance	Providing Clarity
Perspective	Focus primarily on own and organization's success

Employees know what they need to do to make the organization successful | Focus on others, especially on employee success

Employees seek clarity of an uncertain future and clear expectations of their job to thrive |
| **Actions** | No effort expended to discover how to motivate the workforce since they are paid to perform | Find the one reason for the organization's existence and use it as a rallying cry for employee motivation |
| **Consequences** | Organization's workforce slows down due to the uncertainty and possibly negative outlook of the future | Organization's workforce continues at a constant pace to accomplish the clear goal with a positive outlook |

Figure 5: The Value of Providing Clarity

CHAPTER 5

THE VITAL FEW

Pay attention to the vital few and ignore the trivial many.

—John Paul DeJoria

Life is large. We cannot possibly grasp the whole of it in the few years that we have to live. What is vital? What is essential? What may we profitably let go?

—Anna Robertson Brown Lindsay

If we did realize the difference between the vital few and the trivial many in all aspects of our lives, and if we did something about it, we could multiply anything that we valued.

—Richard Koch

I'm going to deviate slightly from my linear discussion of the main concepts that comprise the strengths, clarity and focus approach here to further shorten my new and shorter manager's To-Do list by providing clarity on the "vital few" accelerators of leadership effectiveness, employee engagement, and workforce productivity.

My own research on employee surveys has revealed three

"vital" concepts that great leaders concentrate on to enhance employee productivity and deliver breakthrough business results (Trinka, 2005). Understandably, I honed in on the characteristics that differentiate great leaders from the rest and focus on what's working. As mentioned, I find this approach much more positive than the opposite approach that probes weaknesses and what isn't working. When I reviewed numerous surveys on topics important to employee engagement and productivity, I noticed unusual similarities in findings and recommendations. I viewed these similarities as undeniable and realized that the employees who completed these surveys conscientiously filled them out with the fervent "hope" for positive workplace changes in leadership and culture. I regularly hear employees complain that few things actually change as a result of these survey efforts, so I strived to amplify their voices that eagerly yearn for more effective leadership.

The "vital few" concepts of develops others, results-driven performance, and communication surfaced repeatedly to differentiate leaders who achieved the highest levels of employee engagement and productivity. Specifically, the evidence supported the establishment of a high-performance leadership culture (results-driven performance), not from a command and control perspective, but one that involved the establishment of a learning environment (develops others) with a conscious focus on continuous dialogue within work teams (communication). Furthermore, managers who undertook specific activities related to this approach had a much better chance of achieving "breakthrough" employee performance improvements, leading to "breakthrough" results for the organization. Let's look at this approach more closely.

Develops Others

Few managers would disagree on the importance of their crucial role in coaching and mentoring employees and many spend a considerable amount of their valuable time on employee development activities. Recently, the Corporate Leadership Council's Learning and Development Roundtable analyzed survey responses from nearly 8,500 employees and their managers on a wide range of employee development activities (Corporate Executive Board, 2003). The results confirm that a vast majority of managers (three out of four) agree that coaching and mentoring their employees is crucial to organizational success and report spending about 15–20 percent of their time on employee development activities. However, the results also indicate that employees rate their managers barely above average (4.05 out of 7.0) on their effectiveness in this role. Furthermore, most managers do not see a significant return on their time investment.

Examining the employee-development activities of the highest rated managers revealed that some activities have a much more positive influence on improving employee engagement than others. Statistical estimates show that improving a manager's effectiveness at employee development can positively influence employee retention and satisfaction by as much as 40 percent, commitment by as much as 30 percent, and productivity by as much as 20 percent. The evidence is even more staggering for senior leaders who are the best at developing their subordinate managers. These managers are 25 percent more likely to stay, 33 percent more engaged, give 35 percent more discretionary effort, and experience 27 percent higher employee performance and productivity (Corporate Executive Board, 2003). These are breakthrough results!

Survey responses show some fascinating disparities in perceptions between employees and managers concerning employee development. The vast majority of employees seek to learn and grow in the course of doing day-to-day work and want their managers to create a learning environment in that context. On the other hand, many managers report a lack of confidence to perform well in that role. Armed with the results of this research and organizational support, managers can proceed with much more confidence in performing specifically targeted employee development activities and the business case is compelling.

Leaders should establish an environment and strategy to support continuous on-the-job learning. The good news for busy managers is that employees actually want to learn more on-the-job and blur the line between learning and work. Too often, organizations and managers exclusively focus on external development programs or worse yet; outsource the job of employee development to the organization's internal training division. Leaders need to create an environment where learning flourishes at work. I suggest actions such as handing out work assignments with a clear explanation of why that employee was selected for the task and how they can use or hone their unique talents on it; answering employee questions with a "What do you think?" response instead of a quick answer; and displaying how the organization can best act to meet individual aspirations through collaboration. I again ask you to think of the *best* leader you worked for or with and recall the dialogue you had with that person regarding your development. My experience suggests that most people describe how that leader assigned you to difficult projects and then had considerable confidence and trust in your abilities and set challenging goals for you to develop and realize your full potential.

Results-Driven Performance

All managers agree on the importance of employee productivity and business results and would probably rate themselves fairly proficient in providing performance feedback. Recently, the Corporate Leadership Council's Learning and Development Roundtable analyzed survey responses from nearly 20,000 employees and managers on a wide range of manager-related activities involving employee performance (Corporate Executive Board, 2002). Overall, managers received a poor report card on these activities as only 30–40 percent of employees agreed that their managers clearly communicated performance standards and provided fair and accurate feedback to help them do their jobs better.

Interestingly, most of the performance improvement activities that managers can utilize (e.g., providing specific suggestions for doing the job better, detailing the amount of effort to put into a job, and diffusing unhealthy rivalries and competition, etc.)

have minimal impact on individual employee productivity. The results clearly show that managers have a much better chance of vastly improving employee productivity by targeting their efforts on a much smaller list of activities. In fact, managers who set clear performance standards, become more knowledgeable about employee performance, and provide fair and accurate informal feedback on performance strengths can significantly improve individual employee productivity. And when discussing weaknesses, managers who clearly focus on specific suggestions for improvement or development can improve employee performance. Conversely, those who exclusively emphasize weaknesses most often dramatically decrease performance. In short, managers who provide feedback that is voluntary, detailed, immediate, and positive can significantly increase employee productivity.

This information doesn't surprise us. We've heard it all before and it seems intuitive. However, survey responses again show some disparities in perceptions between employees and managers. The majority of employees believe that formal performance reviews do nothing to actually help their on-the-job performance, yet they crave voluntary and detailed informal performance feedback, especially on strengths. Interestingly, the majority of managers view formal performance reviews as an administrative requirement rather than as an influential lever to positively influence employee productivity. In fact, many managers report that they specifically cite performance weaknesses to lower an employee's rating below the highest mark rather than emphasizing strengths to raise performance ratings above minimally successful. On informal feedback, employees report that most managers provide general praise, rather than specific and detailed recognition.

I don't mean to imply that managers can never mention or speak to employees about weaknesses, in effect being "easy" on them. Again, recall the conversations that you had with the *best* leader you worked for or with. Was that manager easy on you? I mostly hear that great leaders are neither "easy" nor "soft" on their employees. In fact, they're tough on us because they set high standards, yet also show high confidence in our ability to achieve more than we think we can.

Communication

In 1982, Tom Peters and Bob Waterman coined the acronym, MBWA, or management by walking around (Peters and Waterman, 1982). This concept has become so universal that new managers almost instinctively know that they need to "walk around" to achieve high effectiveness levels. Unfortunately, they may not have specific objectives or topics in mind for the conversations they have with their employees while they walk around. In general, that might be all right, but I offer some additional suggestions. Marcus Buckingham (2005) advises managers to seek to turn talent into performance and discover what's unique in each individual and capitalize on it. He also encourages leaders to rally people to a better future by providing clarity on what the organization considers universally important and crucial to its existence (Buckingham, 2005). Such clarity reduces uncertainty concerning the future; reduced uncertainty leads to higher engagement; higher engagement means more effective leadership; and better leadership delivers improved outcomes.

I suggest that leaders need to say, "This is where we're going" (paint a vivid picture of a successful future for the organization and its employees) and specifically cite why he or she needs each person to get there. When I reflect back on my career, I don't recall many instances where I heard this type of message and if I had, I also know what kind of impact it might have had. Imagine a leader vividly and confidently describing the future and then specifically explaining to you why he or she needed you to get there. That would have kept me engaged for months! Again, recall the conversations you've had with the *best* leaders that you worked for or with. That person was likely preoccupied with making us successful and because of that, we did our very best, we committed more of our discretionary effort, we were loyal, and we trusted that he or she had our best interests in mind when making quick decisions without our input. Because of their emphasis on us, we reciprocated with intense productivity and enjoyed it, even though it might have been exhausting.

The "Vital Few" Concepts

The evidence that I cite is coalescing around creating a compelling business case for concentrating effort on only a few managerial and leadership concepts with the most impact relating to developing others, results-driven performance, and communication. However, most people believe that the leadership perspective of their profession is unique and that a shorter list of "vital few" leadership concepts does not completely apply to their environment. Upon further review of various employee surveys and managerial 360-degree assessments, I've discovered that the similarities among various professions' leadership perspectives far outweigh whatever minimal differences might exist. For others, this approach either seems too simple or appears to offer little new insight. I quickly point out that although my "vital few" concepts might appear simplistic or rudimentary; my experience tells me that employees don't rate managers very high in these three concepts. That same Merit Systems Protection Board (MSPB) survey I referenced earlier found that less than half of over 37,000 federal employees view their supervisors as a resource for improving workplace skills (Rutzick, 2006). Another recent government-wide survey revealed that only 41 percent of employees view their organization's leaders effective at generating workforce motivation and commitment (U.S. Office of Personnel Management, 2016).

As a result, I have formulated a visual depiction of my research conclusions (Figure 6 on the next page) that displays the relationships among what I view as foundational leadership concepts, the "vital few" accelerators, and the outcomes that we're all interested in. In general, I believe great leadership is characterized by the possession of a few foundational leadership concepts of personal character, such as integrity and honesty, self assurance, professionalism, and service motivation, which serve as critical selection criteria and probably cannot be improved much by leadership training.

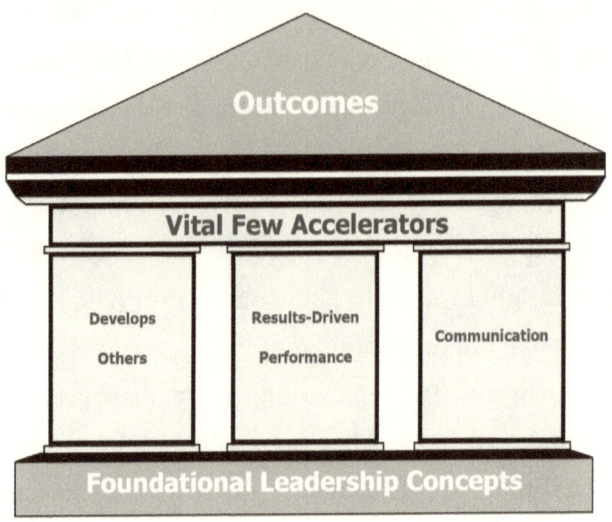

Figure 6: Manager's New and Shorter To-Do List

Few would argue the belief that a strong and solid base of personal character must underlie leaders in every profession. Some highly publicized cases of a leader's lack of integrity have recently undermined the credibility of leadership in general and left a lasting impression of the great importance of personal character. In their study of over 25,000 public and private sector managers, Jack Zenger and Joe Folkman (2002) found that displaying personal character through high integrity and honesty forms the basis of strong leadership and acts like the center pole of a tent that leaders must raise prior to and higher than the outer poles of leadership characteristics.

Great leaders use this foundation as a solid base and apply a "vital few" accelerators to achieve the outcomes crucial to their organization's success. For example, by focusing on improving the behaviors associated with "Develops Others," "Results-driven Performance," and "Communication," managers can increase overall leadership effectiveness scores by 50–60 percent. The essential leadership actions associated with these concepts are: 1) creates an environment and strategy to support continuous on-the-job learning, 2) clarifies performance expectations and gives timely, constructive feedback on tasks and assignments, and 3) strategically uses communication to produce enthusiasm and foster an atmosphere of open exchange, support, and trust. This research cites considerable evidence that clarity, when used intentionally and specifically, produces the desired outcomes of high employee engagement and productivity. Leaders effective at applying the "vital few" accelerators clearly gain the perception of "great" leadership in the eyes of their employees.

Common Activities Associated with the "Vital Few"

An overwhelming body of evidence exists to highlight the important and vital role of a manager's leadership competencies on employee productivity and retention. I have shown evidence on the value of focusing on a "vital few" accelerating competencies to engender increased employee productivity and business results. I realize that these competencies represent more general concepts than specific recommendations on potentially useful activities, so I will offer some practical advice as well. Questions often arise about which managerial activities have the most impact on improving employee performance and what the extent of that improvement is. However, the potential list of activities that a manager can undertake to improve employee performance and productivity is as long as the oceans are wide. Thus, I evaluate a long list of managerial activities to determine the much smaller number of those activities that have the most impact on improving both employee productivity and leadership effectiveness, ultimately achieving dramatic increases in organizational results. While the approach of finding "what's working" to lead organizational change is not new, the application of this focus to leadership assessment and development is relatively new.

After reviewing the impact of over 250 possible managerial activities, I suggest a short list of only 12 that have the most potential for delivering high employee productivity improvement, since these differentiate great leaders from the rest. By studying success and recognizing and appreciating what works for great leaders, we can determine the actions that have the most impact on both employee productivity and leadership effectiveness. And the best news is that busy managers may be able to decrease emphasis on some of the activities we have done in the past that have the least impact. In other words, we can create "Stop Doing" lists to supplement our edited "To-Do" lists to ensure that the remaining activities have maximum impact.

Given the vast range of responsibilities and activities that managers can undertake, any method of simplifying a time-pressed manager's life is worthwhile, especially with specific evidence in support of a few key concepts. In that light, I have summarized the results of the previously cited surveys around the common themes that emerge involving employee development, employee performance, and communication. Figure 7 depicts the most influential activities, grouped by these three vital themes in descending order of their impact on a combined index of employee engagement and leadership effectiveness. Overall, activities involving employee development have the highest average impact on employee productivity and leadership effectiveness at 33.3 percent, employee performance averages 28.5 percent, and communication comes in a close third at 25.7 percent.

Employee Development	Employee Performance	Communication
Leaders act as good role models for developing employees.	Leader is knowledgeable about employee performance.	Leaders genuinely listen to employees and value their opinions (dialogue).
Leaders encourage employee development and make it a priority.	Leaders provide voluntary, detailed, immediate, and positive informal feedback.	Leaders clearly communicate expectations and standards.
Leaders ensure each project or assignment is a learning experience for employees.	Leaders recognize and emphasize employee strengths.	Leaders pass along job and development opportunities.
Leaders help employees apply new skills and knowledge on-the-job.	Leaders regularly appreciate employee contributions and accomplishment.	Leaders share information employees need to understand and trust the organization.

Figure 7: Most Influential Managerial Activities

Great leaders provide a confident and vivid description of successful end goals and determine ways to assess progress and celebrate wins along the way. They assign the right people to the right task to turn talent into performance and figure out how to develop existing skill gaps on-the-job. And finally, they connect the dots for employees by showing how the work supports the organization's mission and vision, how it will develop participants, and how everyone's opinion will count.

CHAPTER 6

APPLYING FOCUS

If you spend your life trying to be good at everything, you will never be great at anything.

—Tom Rath

The key to mastery is simplicity. Commit to a monomaniacal focus and practice only a few things. Build your life around the vital few. Distraction dilutes your genius.

—Robin Sharma

You are more likely to acquire power by narrowing your focus and applying your energies, like the sun's rays, to a limited range of activities in a small number of domains.

—Jeffrey Pfeffer

Great leaders are almost always great simplifiers, who can cut through argument, debate, and doubt to offer a solution everybody can understand.

—General Colin Powell

The third and final item on the very short manager's To-Do list I'm presenting to you deals with applying focus to ensure both meaningful and important results for your organization.

Results versus "Busyness"

Earlier, I asked if you felt busy at work. Undoubtedly, yes was your quick answer. To me, it seems like how busy you are has become the standard of success. We all feel like we have to remain very busy to let our supervisors know that we are still valuable. This is apparent when your annual performance appraisal comes around and your supervisor asks you to complete a self-assessment or review of your work for the past year. I've seen many employees draft pages and pages of things they've done although many times our supervisors restrict us to a one page maximum. So, do we use normal margins and font or do we squeeze the margins and decrease the font size so that we can stuff as much as we can on that one page? Some performance plan software programs maniacally limit the characters we can use on our self assessments, thus further frustrating our efforts. Why do we have the tendency to show that we were busy and completed massive quantities of work? Why wouldn't we just cite our 3 or 4 major accomplishments for the year that were meaningful to the organization? My answer is that the common notion of "busyness" has become the standard of success and we all must show our supervisors how busy we've been.

Have you ever noticed the senior leadership in your

organization touting major accomplishments when they occur? It sometimes seems like these celebrations are definitely too few and far between. And the celebrations really herald the leader who accomplished these major results and they use glorified language that seems to put that person on a high pedestal. They may even call him/her a great leader! Perhaps they even have the accomplished leader stand on a pedestal! And the celebration sometimes even touts the accomplishment more than the leader as if the results were vastly more important. I truly believe that senior leadership is actually quite grateful that someone has actually accomplished something of note. I've been at ceremonies like this where the results didn't seem like great accomplishments that moved the organization forward. To me, it seems as though the senior leadership so rarely sees results that they can't wait to crow about it even when the impact isn't that extraordinary! Certainly, I've *never* seen a ceremony where senior leadership congratulates a leader or calls him/her "great" for being the busiest in the organization! So, if senior leadership highly values actual results, why are so many of us still chasing "busyness?"

I've noticed a few things that I do at work that remind me of the importance of results over "busyness." Often, I personally make duplicates of presentations, reports, and other documents on a copy machine and send copies of documents over the phone with a fax machine. I catch myself waiting for the machine to complete its work and I know I have many other things I should accomplish while the copy or fax operation is underway. But, I can't help myself to stand there and watch the machine do its work. I've come to the conclusion that I'm simply amazed that

I'm actually seeing results occur right before my eyes and I'm compelled to watch the process!

Another fixation I have is over email, especially after an extended time away for travel or vacation when I see a very high number of unread messages. As I'm attempting to catch up, I notice myself merely reading messages that call for action on my part and moving on to the next message before I take that action. I press right through until I've turned all my unread messages into read ones and changed either the color of the font or changed it from bold to normal print. I actually feel a sense of accomplishment when I've read all those unread emails even though I still have tons of work to do to complete the actions that some of those messages have called for. Again, I think that I'm more satisfied in my sense of accomplishment of "catching up" from an extended absence by reading all my email rather than completing all the work that I missed while I was away!

Most Important Competency for the 21st Century

I usually ask my audience in the presentations I give what they think is the most important competency of the 21st century. I get many answers such as critical thinking, analytical reasoning, agility, communication, problem solving, etc. Certainly, all those attributes are very important for current leaders, but I tend to think differently about the question. I maintain that to achieve the results that our organizations need to thrive, we need to focus our efforts on just a few (or one) task at a time and see it through to completion. Remember that senior leadership heralds a leader who actually accomplishes something? So apparently, the best advice is to focus you and your staff's efforts on achieving results important for the organization.

I remember my time in the FAA and the organization's practice of setting a number of important goals for each year. That seems like a laudable practice; however, usually the number of "important" results to achieve in the upcoming year numbered at least thirty! Who could possibly focus on thirty goals each year? The FAA did something more with these goals though by making them public and printing out a glossy-page pamphlet describing each of the thirty-plus goals and calling it "The Flight Plan." Nice touch! The organization actually used these goals for calibrating senior executive performance by confirming performance bonuses with a percentage of the goals achieved that year. The organization lowered senior executive performance bonuses if the percentage of goals achieved went below ninety percent. I remember one year that the organization achieved twenty-seven of its thirty goals so we were all happy that our performance bonuses would remain fully intact. However, I then considered the three goals that we didn't achieve revolved around aviation safety, financial management, and contract management. You might think that those three goals would have utmost importance to an organization that existed to ensure the safety of private and commercial air travel. Some organizations plan incessantly to outline important goals, but need to pay close attention to the total number of "breakthrough initiatives" and how it rewards its workforce upon achievement of those goals.

Many people express great pride in their ability to "multi-task" as if that is a quality that we all need to possess to succeed. Apparently, these people can increase their "busyness" quotient by multi-tasking and feel that focus just isn't that important. I'm certain you've seen drivers on the road attempting to multi-task by using their cell phones, eating, searching for channels on their satellite radio, or applying makeup. We all know how dangerous those behaviors are and have seen the spike in car accidents recently due to distracted driving habits. Most states now have laws that govern distracted driving and restrict activities that would otherwise interfere with a driver's concentration on driving.

Recently, I attended a conference where one of the keynote speeches was on multi-tasking (Hunter, 2016). Initially, I thought that the speaker would laud the practice, but I was surprised when he actually cited considerable research and analytical studies that demonstrated humanity's inability to effectively multi-task. He then proceeded to demonstrate the analytical results to the audience by first having us attempt to complete a task under normal conditions. The task wasn't easy and required considerable focus to complete on time, which a few of us did. Then he introduced other inputs that we had to process in our mind at the same time that we were attempting to perform a task similar to the first. Actually, none of us came close to completing the task and this demonstration drove home an important lesson for me. I had always known that I wasn't very effective when I tried to multi-task and now there was ample qualitative and quantitative research supporting the fact that humans don't multi-task well... whew! Was I ever relieved! But, how can we apply this lesson in organizational leadership? I believe we need to focus on multiple finished tasks rather than multi-tasking. And we shouldn't diffuse our efforts over a great number of areas. We need to focus on the vital few issues extremely important to the organization.

The Impact of Focus for Leaders

I will illustrate the effectiveness of focus on organizational results by relating a story of an example that happened during my time in the IRS. The organization at the time had just adopted the new Gallup Q12™ employee engagement survey (Buckingham and Coffman, 1999). The decision was reached jointly through a strong labor-management partnership present at that time. After the survey was over and the analysis complete, Gallup came in to deliver a presentation on the results of the survey. As survey organizations typically do, Gallup presented a multitude of data that was generally focused on the lowest scoring questions and the lowest scoring business units of the organization. I call these depictions skyscraper charts as we see the highest to lowest scoring questions or business units shown in one graph and the overall chart looks a series of skyscrapers. Of course, our eyes immediately focus on the lowest scoring question or business unit. The presentation didn't really focus on what the organization should do with the mountains of data generated by the analysis, I guess most survey organizations justify their existence by the complexity of the report they issue after administering an employee survey. In other words, how "busy" is the report? Many of the business unit heads who attended the meeting left scratching their heads thinking about what they should do in response to the employee feedback. Instinctively, they knew that the employees just provided valuable feedback to the organization in the fervent hope that the senior leaders would do something as a result.

The head of the largest business unit in the IRS then turned to me to ask for help interpreting the results and creating an action plan to address the issues raised in the survey. That business unit processed the roughly 150 million tax returns submitted by U.S. taxpayers through ten processing centers throughout the country and in two large data centers for electronically filed returns. The work in these centers amounted to little more than factory assembly lines where quite a bit of repetitive menial labor was performed to move the return from envelope opening to processed return. I remembered visiting one of these centers and until you have seen what one million paper tax returns looks like loaded in wheeled carts lining the hallways, you have no concept of the amount of work performed at these processing centers.

At one step of the process, I talked with the person who put a tax return number on every return, which was essential for tracking it to completion. After many failed attempts at automating this process, the only effective method was to stamp each return with one of those hand-held stamping machines that automatically rolls to the next number after stamping out a number. That person had a performance standard of stamping about 1,000 returns per day and you can imagine that task doesn't lend itself to high employee engagement. Many other functions had similar menial tasks, so it was no wonder why this business unit had placed second from the bottom among the nine IRS business units on employee engagement.

I needed to analyze the survey responses more closely to find a way to focus improvement efforts on issues that really drove employee engagement in this unit. I asked the business unit head if I could analyze the responses in the aggregate without any knowledge of who submitted them and he agreed. So, I studied the results of over 80,000 respondents in that business unit and discovered that only four of the twelve survey questions differentiated the best workgroups (top ten percent) from the rest. Yes, I analyzed managers who generated the highest survey scores to discover what drove high levels of employee engagement in those workgroups. Similar to the results of previously cited research and surveys, managers have a much better chance of vastly improving the workplace environment for their employees by targeting efforts on a much smaller list of successful performance drivers. By listing the four key differentiating survey questions, I clearly saw patterns of what survey respondents are telling their managers to focus on to achieve success. In no particular order, the four survey questions that the best managers were focusing on to achieve high engagement in their workgroups were:

- In the last seven days, I have received recognition or praise for doing good work.
- At work, my opinions seem to count.
- There is someone at work who encourages my development.
- This last year, I have had opportunities at work to learn and grow.

The first two questions relate to conversations about performance and the next two speak directly to the value of employee development activities and communication to establish an atmosphere of open exchange and support, thus validating the "vital few accelerators" approach I had discovered in my earlier research. The workgroups who achieved high employee engagement scores (in the top ten percent) also delivered high levels of on-the-job productivity. Similarly, the Gallup researchers, Marcus Buckingham and Curt Coffman (1999), found that in one retail chain, workgroups who scored in the top twenty-five percent on engagement ended the year almost five percent over their sales budget while those scoring in the bottom twenty-five percent were nearly one percent below budget, which amounted to a difference of 140 million dollars. Profit/loss sheets and employee turnover comparisons pointed to an even more dramatic impact of scoring in the top twenty-five percent on employee engagement (Buckingham and Coffman, 1999).

Armed with the results of my research, I scheduled time with the business unit head to create an action plan for improvement. After I explained my analysis and showed the results, he asked what he should do. I calmly replied that he should pick one of these four differentiating questions to focus on for the next year until the next survey. He was a bit shocked and asked which one and I contended that he just needed to pick one of these four and focus on it for the entire year and it didn't really matter which one. In effect, the choice was much less important than the focus. He agreed and chose to focus on the second of the four differentiating questions asking: "At work, my opinions seem to count."

He then set off to effectively focus on this question. He worked hard and effectively communicated this message hundreds of times throughout the year and had workgroups all the way down to the frontline level conduct action planning meetings to focus on this area and elevate any issues that they couldn't resolve locally to higher leadership levels. Considerable effort up and down the organization occurred throughout the year to communicate the importance of this issue to the organization. Many ideas sprung out of these sessions that served to streamline processes for efficiency and cost effectiveness. During the tax filing season that year, the business unit experienced its best activity and outcome measures to date in all categories.

The Gallup Q12™ survey was administered again the next year and everyone anxiously awaited the results. Not surprisingly, the aforementioned business unit moved up from second to the bottom to second to the top and the percentage increase in employee engagement was the highest one-year gain of any comparably-sized organization in Gallup's database! That, my friends, is the power of focus! And it also seems that the focus itself has more significance than the choice of what to focus on.

Another example of the power of focus was when I was with the FAA. After my first couple of years there, Ray LaHood became the new Secretary of Transportation. After seeing that the Department of Transportation consistently scored in the bottom three Federal government agencies for employee engagement and the FAA scored 214 among 215 subordinate government organizations, he proclaimed that he wanted to become the number one government agency in employee engagement. A big, hairy, audacious goal to be sure! Although he didn't consult with me on his choice of actions, he decided to follow a similar approach by focusing on suggested improvements by employees. He talked about this approach incessantly at every opportunity and created an "Idea Hub" software system to gather employee input and opinion. And then he created an office to read each suggestion and staff it out to the appropriate part of the Transportation Department for action under his signature. I remember receiving many of these questions and I was always pressed for my response to the employee's suggestion. We were allowed to disagree, but we had to cite substantial evidence for why the proposed idea wouldn't work. The focus on this issue continued throughout his tenure as Transportation Secretary and he achieved amazing results. The Department of Transportation moved into the top ten government agencies in employee engagement and remains there today. Again, I don't know if this is the right issue to focus on, but clearly the focus was more important to achieving results than the choice itself.

Martial Arts Focus

I practice martial arts and as it turns out, I started this effort much too late in life. My story was that I had spent the first twenty-five years of my career going to school and learning as much as I could, both in degree programs and in various training courses. I promised myself that after I completed my doctorate degree, I would stop concentrating on my mind and start to focus on developing my body and I aspired to become an accomplished martial artist. As it turns out, martial arts is all about developing body, mind, and spirit in the art of self defense and I appreciated the rigor of this approach and how much it can improve your entire life.

I practice Hapkido, a Korean martial art, that integrates the study of striking, avoiding and blocking, joint locking, holding, throwing, weapons, internal techniques (meditation, breathing, internal energy development), and healing. Loosely translated, Hapkido means the "art of coordinated power." Physical techniques are characterized by a constant flow of striking, blocking, holding, and throwing techniques. Constant motion and fluid circular movements are designed to blend with an opponent's force. Tactics often alternate between highly aggressive and defensive modes, with power being generated through use of one's entire body. Techniques can involve either large or small circular motions, depending on tactics. Initially, I attempted to study all aspects of the art collectively, hoping to progressively improve my techniques. It wasn't until I realized that I couldn't "multi-task" my way to expertise in Hapkido; I had to focus on integrating my efforts through power or Ki as the Koreans call it throughout all my techniques. Coordination and power (or Ki) were the keys to focus on, instead of every specific aspect of the art. Hapkido is all about how to effectively defend yourself and use the opponent's force in your favor. Finally, Hapkido philosophy, like the philosophies of many martial arts, emphasizes the integration of mind, body, and spirit; the perfection of human character; social responsibility; and the appropriate use of force.

I had a difficult time choosing the right martial art to study and I visited many schools in my endeavor to select the right one. In one school, instructors gauged the effectiveness of striking techniques by having students break boards with their hands, elbows, and feet. To me, that seemed more offensive that defensive, so when I eventually made my final selection of the school and art that I was to study four years after obtaining my doctorate degree, I mentioned to the master (*Sabumnim* in Korean) that I hoped we weren't going to break boards or anything else in class. Of course, on the first day of class after our warm-ups and basic technique practice, you can probably guess what Phan Sabumnim asked the class to do...yes break a small piece of wood with a neck chop strike! He successfully demonstrated the technique and the students spent the remainder of the class time attempting to break that piece of wood. We all failed and were given a homework assignment to successfully break that board before the next class. I completed my homework assignment and at the end of the next class, we attempted to break a slightly larger piece of wood with a hammer fist strike. I had learned a little about focusing power during my homework assignment and really focused my entire body's power into the blow, emanating from my core. I was one of only two students who were able to break the board that night.

Interestingly, I discovered that I had overcome my initial anxiety to this practice and now found that the process of generating and then focusing Ki or power during the execution of Hapkido techniques was the key towards mastering the art. I endeavored to advance this knowledge by competing in wood and concrete breaking events in numerous martial arts tournaments across the United States and abroad. Many of these tournaments were organized by the United States/World Breaking Association (USBA/WBA). As I gained experience, I learned that I was very competitive among the many martial artists who participated in these events and I actually enjoyed it. The USBA/WBA awards "Competitor of the Year" status to the martial artist who accumulates the most points by winning events at these tournaments. For nearly three years from the beginning of 2012 until the middle of 2014, I was the number one breaker in the U.S. among adult males. And I was competing in my late fifties with teenagers and twenty-somethings. Again, I relate this story not to boast my accomplishments, but to drive home the effectiveness of focused power and energy. Believe me, the focused power required to break a stack of a dozen or more boards or concrete slabs is significant and when you discover how to achieve that focus, it is truly mind over matter.

Remember that Ed, the director of the information technology center in my first example, focused leadership development efforts on strategic thinking, technical credibility, and developing others to achieve breakthrough improvements and ward off closure of his facility. Recall the focus that my father demanded of both of his sons in the course of working on the farm to ensure the best results...in this case, prolific grain harvests. Consider how IRS employees used the clarity of "We Fund America" to focus efforts of ensuring the best customer service and tax compliance possible. How about the focus applied by FAA senior leadership when they demanded that I get the issue of hiring and training many thousands of air traffic controllers "off the front page of the Washington Post?" Also, recollect how corporations such as Microsoft and Apple provide clarity and apply focus for their employees respectively by emphasizing the power of great deals and challenging the status quo by thinking differently.

I want to revisit one last thing that I reviewed earlier to emphasize how applying focus can really add significant value to both work and life. I mentioned earlier that the Merit Systems Protection Board (MSPB) recently administered a Federal government-wide employee survey and one of the question results revealed that 98 percent of Federal government employees were motivated by pride in their work (Rutzick, 2006). That seems pretty simple…make employees more proud of their work and they are motivated to do more of it! Talk about focus!

Figure 8 summarizes the differences between diffusing effort across many issues and applying focus on only a few or one:

	Diffusing Effort	Applying Focus
Perspective	"Busyness" is the standard of success	Achieving a few results important to the organization ensures success
	Multi-tasking allows me to seem even more busy	Focus on completing multiple finished tasks, usually one at a time
	The correct choice of what's important to an organization trumps the focus itself	The focus itself and the intensity and completeness of that focus is more important than choosing correctly
Actions	Select many different factors to consider when defining organizational success	Clearly define organizational success with only a few... or one...factor and maintain that focus over time
Consequences	Organization's workforce is confused on what defines performance and success in the organization	Organization's workforce focuses on the single issue deemed important and delivers outstanding and meaningful results

Figure 8: Diffusing Effort vs. Applying Focus

CHAPTER 7

SUMMARY

We are what we repeatedly do; excellence, then, is not an act, but a habit.

—Aristotle

We are made wise, not by the recollection of our past, but by the responsibility for our future.

—Bernard Shaw

The successful warrior is the average man, with laser-like focus.

—Bruce Lee

Focus on what you are doing now to breakthrough your performance!

—Jensen Siaw

In this book, I've described the strengths, clarity, and focus approach as a simple, yet effective way of accomplishing work and achieving breakthrough results. I encouraged you to break out of our similar thinking patterns and really think differently on how to solve problems. I described each aspect of the strengths, clarity, and focus approach through both illuminating stories and focused research. Hopefully, the business case for adopting this approach is self-evident, yet I want to provide you with some more statistical evidence in Figure 9 that may further strengthen your resolve to attempt it. Managers who leverage strengths, provide clarity, and apply focus for their workforce have employees who are much more likely to stay, more satisfied, more committed, and more productive than those who don't.

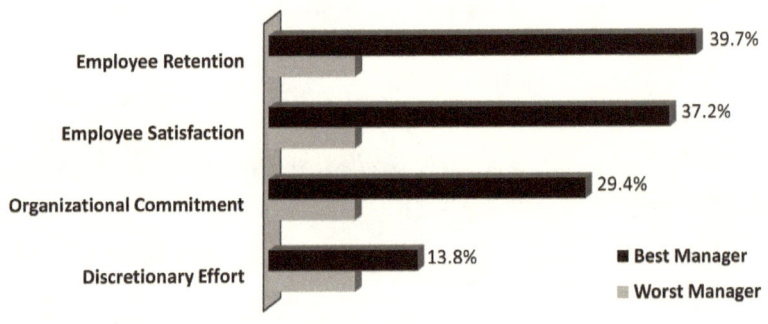

Figure 9: Outcomes for Strengths, Clarity, and Focus Approach

Executives and senior managers who have subordinate managers generate even higher levels of engagement and commitment (33 percent), resulting in performance improvement of up to 27 percent! This adds some numbers to my Figure 1 in Chapter 2 where I didn't show specific numbers regarding how much the leveraging strengths approach outperforms the correcting weaknesses approach. I figured that if I would have cited these levels of improvement then, your skepticism would have heightened and you may not have believed me. Does this make sense to you? I believe I've made a sound business case for this approach, but perhaps you may consider that what I'm saying is incorrect? Was I at least clear? As we learned in the Chapter 6, the focus itself is often more important than the correct choice.

Fifty years ago, Peter Drucker wrote in *The Effective Executive* (1967) that the best organizations and managers "gather their strengths together and make their weaknesses irrelevant." Certainly, back then he was well ahead of his time and with the Total Quality Management process improvement technique in vogue at the time, his advice fell mostly on deaf ears. Today however, we can add much more experience, especially with knowledge workers, and added statistical evidence to make a better case. I'm not saying that the correcting weaknesses problem solving approach is wrong, I'm merely encouraging thinking differently to leverage strengths to achieve breakthrough performance improvement. Clarity reduces uncertainty; less uncertainty means more commitment; more commitment results in more engagement; and more engagement means better business results! The *best* leaders provide that clarity! And finally, focus on multiple finished tasks rather than "multi-tasking."

I have done a considerable amount of research on leadership and organizational performance and I'll cite some of that now centering on high-performance leadership culture and legacy impact. Leaders can elicit a high-performance leadership culture specifically by thinking differently to discover what's working in organizations and leveraging those strengths, providing clarity of purpose, and applying focus to achieve meaningful and breakthrough results for the organization. All organizations place high emphasis on recruiting and developing high-performance leaders, yet confusion ensues when deciding on the competencies or characteristics to use in the effort. Leaders create legacies in organizations, whether they intend to or not and I offer the strengths, clarity, and focus approach to guide organizations on both these issues.

High-Performance Leadership Culture

Facing a continuing competitive economic environment and intense scrutiny of leadership bench strength, most organizations currently place great emphasis on succession management and plan to increase investment in leadership development. Nowadays, organizations increasingly require effective leaders to move forward, regardless of sector (public, private, or non-profit), industry, or cyclical economic and budget fluctuations. Recently, Accenture (Corporate Executive Board, 2003) surveyed over 1,000 CEOs and discovered that five of the top seven corporate priorities related to workforce and leadership quality (Figure 10 on next page). In addition, the President's Management Agenda (2016) cites the importance of leadership as a crucial driver of strategic government human capital management.

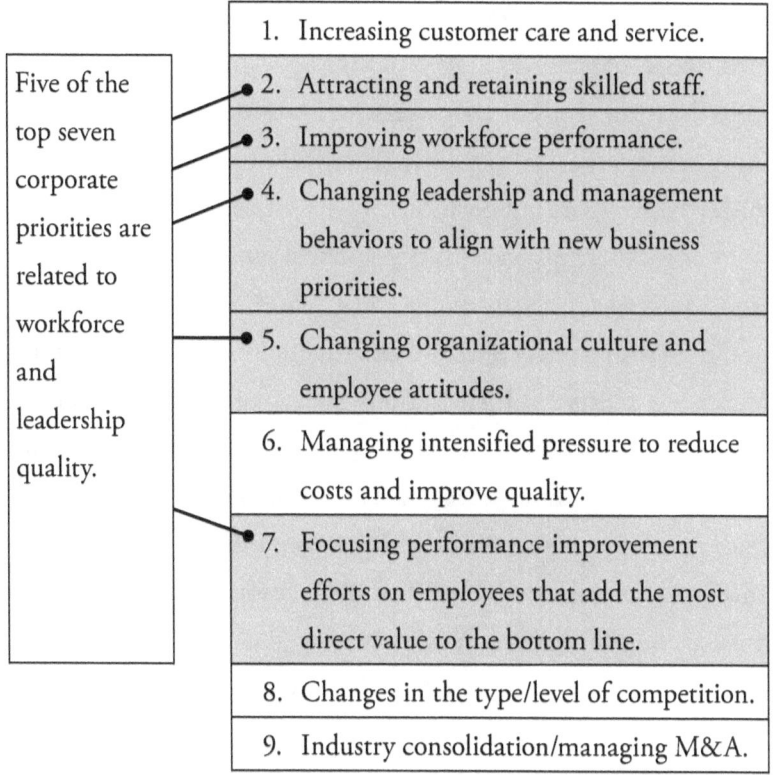

Five of the top seven corporate priorities are related to workforce and leadership quality.	1. Increasing customer care and service.
	• 2. Attracting and retaining skilled staff.
	• 3. Improving workforce performance.
	• 4. Changing leadership and management behaviors to align with new business priorities.
	• 5. Changing organizational culture and employee attitudes.
	6. Managing intensified pressure to reduce costs and improve quality.
	• 7. Focusing performance improvement efforts on employees that add the most direct value to the bottom line.
	8. Changes in the type/level of competition.
	9. Industry consolidation/managing M&A.

Figure 10: Top Corporate Strategic Priorities

Unfortunately, the near-universal agreement about the criticality of leadership is not matched by universal agreement among organizations on how to develop effective leaders. If leadership development is so important, why is there such a lack of consensus about how to effectively achieve it? Most organizations comment that they have too few "great" leaders to address the challenge of executive succession, insufficient resources for creating an effective leadership development strategy, and an incomplete understanding of what issues to focus on. Ironically, the challenge facing organizations to design and implement an effective leadership development strategy is not a lack of viable ideas but the converse, an overwhelming number of plausible ideas and approaches and little empirical or systematic evidence with which to sort out decisions.

I seek to help organizations make sense of this baffling landscape and allocate (or reallocate) scarce leadership development resources to optimally establish and maintain a high-performance leadership culture. Organizations shouldn't have to choose a leadership development strategy based on intuition and anecdotal evidence. They should base decisions for building the desired leadership culture on empirical evidence rather than guesswork, anecdotes, or hunches. Due to limited resources, organizations must make the right choices to develop their leaders, optimally focusing their scarce time, effort, and monetary resources on the point of greatest return. And that's exactly what the strengths, clarity, and focus approach offers on this confusing issue combined with emphasis on the "vital few" accelerators.

So, I've attempted to demonstrate that by focusing on a "vital few" competencies with their associated recommended behaviors, organizations can greatly improve both workforce and leadership quality, which is very high on the list of CEO top priorities and for good reason. In their excellent work, *When Teams Work Best*, Frank LaFasto and Carl Larson (2001) show that companies with "top tier" leadership quality ("great" leaders) outperform their competitors in revenue margins by over 500 percent, in net income by over 700 percent, and in stock price performance by over 800 percent! As we suspected, a manager's, or maybe we should say a leader's, role does have a significant impact on employee productivity and I'm offering the specific, empirically-justified strengths, clarity, and focus approach for improvement. It seems we can use hard science to help apply and build the soft skill of leadership!

Legacy Impact

The paradox at the heart of organizational leadership is that the leader must add value to the organization and not take that away when he or she leaves. An essential part of a leader's job is to become dispensable through creating a *leadership culture* that extends throughout the organization. When an organization becomes incapable of sustaining high performance and falls apart after the leader departs, the subsequent ruin is, in a sense, a validation of that leader's talent and evidence of the value added during his or her tenure. But it is also evidence of that leader's failure to endow the organization with the qualities needed to transcend previous achievements, to nurture the conditions under which leadership can flourish, and to leave a leadership legacy behind. Some leaders fail to create a leadership culture, and instead foster a personal cult. A cult is a rudimentary, incomplete, and inherently short-lived phenomenon that fades when the personality that creates it departs. A culture is much more durable and robust than a cult, because its survival and power do not depend on the presence and personality of a single individual.

Ed's effort to leverage his managements team's strengths, clarify expectations for leadership development efforts at all levels, and focus on inclusion through communication grew roots in the organization and even after he left, the change was embedded in the culture—a legacy. In Ed's new assignment in research and development, he brought a leadership approach of developing products and services in the lap of the customer—a new legacy. And he continues his focus on developing others.

I'll relate one last story regarding the whole concept of thinking differently. I usually return back to the thinking differently concept since it really is at the heart of understanding the strengths, clarity, and focus approach to life and work. While I was in graduate school at The George Washington University, a professor named Jerry Harvey taught many insightful classes and was always popular with his students (a novel concept). When we think of cheating in a school context, we conjure up images in our heads about students talking to each other during exams or looking over another student's shoulder to see their exam answer sheet. I guess that's the "normal" interpretation of cheating. Well, Professor Harvey examined those same conjured-up images and saw students helping each other in a crisis and then established his own definition of cheating as "*not* helping each other in a crisis."

Professor Harvey clung to his own definition of cheating and then demanded that students never cheat in his class. In other words, he never wanted his students to exhibit the behavior of "*not* helping each other in a crisis." He explained this concept on the first day of all of his classes each semester and handed each student a written memo that contained his own definition of cheating and also wrote that he wouldn't tolerate cheating in his classes and if he caught anyone cheating, he would promptly expel that student from his class with a failing grade! Well, you can probably guess what happened next. Of course, one of the students couldn't tolerate Professor Harvey's odd behavior and reported this story to the Dean and gave the Dean a copy of the memo that Professor Harvey handed out.

Obviously, this put the Dean in a precarious position since he was now cornered into doing something about the situation. So, he decided to call Professor Harvey into his office for a chat. As Professor Harvey walked into the Dean's office, the Dean asked him to sit down and then showed Professor Harvey the memo. The Dean asked Professor Harvey if he wrote the memo and handed it out to his students. Professor Harvey quickly replied "yes!" The Dean looked Professor Harvey in the eyes and said: "Can you imagine the chaos that would break out around here if people would start helping each other in a crisis?" Before Professor Harvey could reply, the Dean thought for a moment, scratched his head and said: "Did I say what I think I just said?" Professor Harvey answered that question with another enthusiastic "yes." After a moment of uncomfortable silence, the Dean said: "We'll have to discontinue this meeting now and reconvene at a later date." I guess I use that story as an analogy to extend the question: "Can you imagine the chaos that would break out around here if people would start thinking differently?"

CHAPTER 8

APPLYING THE APPROACH

If your actions inspire others to dream more, learn more, do more, and become more, you are a leader.

—John Quincy Adams

Knowing is not enough. We must apply. Willing is not enough. We must do.

—Bruce Lee

A s you reflect on the concepts that I raised in this book, what might you do differently in either your life and/or work environment? Do you feel you can use the strengths, clarity, and focus approach in any situation to think differently and achieve breakthrough results? Today, we certainly face great challenges—also known as "wicked problems"— and unbelievable complexity, and we need a simple, yet effective way to manage these situations. On the next page, I'll offer you a checklist of sorts to articulate your lessons learned from this book, which I call learning nuggets, how you will craft them into your new leadership strategy, your already existing strengths in adopting this approach that you are aware of, and space to document an action plan to fully implement the characteristics of this approach. See Figure 11 for the details and I believe when you write this down and refer to it often, not only will you become a "great" leader, but also others will perceive you as such and succeed as a result.

Concept or Action	Notes
What are my specific learning nuggets from this book?	
How will my learning nuggets redefine my leadership strategy?	
How will I share my new leadership strategy with others and seek advice for improvement?	
How will I incorporate the advice from others into my new leadership strategy?	
Which parts of the strengths, clarity, and focus approach am I already strong in?	
Which of the "vital few" leadership competencies of developing others, results-driven performance, and communication am I already strong in?	

Concept or Action	Notes
How can I leverage my strengths in this new approach and in the "vital few" competencies to achieve breakthrough results?	
What is the one thing that I can provide clarity to my employees that will reduce the uncertainty of the future?	
Which area will I apply focus on to deliver a meaningful result for the organization?	
How will I share this action plan with my team and supervisor to clearly define success for all?	

Figure 11: Strengths, Clarity, and Focus Action Plan

REFERENCES AND OTHER READINGS

Abrashoff, Captain Michael. *It's Your Ship*. New York, NY: Time Warner, 2002.

Achor, Shawn. *The Happiness Advantage: The Seven Principles of Positive Psychology That Fuel Success and Performance at Work*. New York, NY: Random House, 2010.

American Customer Satisfaction Index (ACSI). "2016 Customer Satisfaction Ratings of U.S. organizations." University of Michigan: www.theacsi.org, 2016.

Avolio, Bruce, and Fred Lulthaus. *The High Impact Leader: Moments Matter in Accelerating Authentic Leadership Development*. New York, NY: McGraw Hill, 2006.

Badaracco, Joseph. *Defining Moments: When Managers Must Choose Between Right and Right*. Boston, MA: Harvard Business Review Press, 1997.

Badaracco, Joseph. *Leading Quietly: An Unorthodox Guide to Doing the Right Thing*. Boston, MA: Harvard Business Review Press, 2002.

Badaracco, Joseph. *Managing in the Gray: Five Timeless Questions for Resolving Your Toughest Problems at Work.* Boston, MA: Harvard Business Review Press, 2016.

Brooks, Martha, Julie Stark, and Sarah Caverhill. *Your Leadership Legacy: The Difference You Make in People's Lives.* San Francisco, CA: Berrett-Koehler Publishers, 2004.

Buckingham, Marcus and Curtis Coffman. *First Break all the Rules: What the World's Greatest Managers Do Differently.* New York, NY: Simon and Schuster, 1999.

Buckingham, Marcus and Donald Clifton. *Now Discover Your Strengths.* New York, NY: The Free Press, 2001.

Buckingham, Marcus. *The One Thing You Need to Know ... About Great Managing, Great Leading, and Sustained Individual Success.* New York, NY: The Free Press, 2005.

Buckingham, Marcus. *StandOut 2.0: Assess your Strengths, Find Your Edge, Win at Work.* Boston, MA: Harvard Business Review Press, 2015.

Charan, Ram, Stephen Drotter, and James Noel. *The Leadership Pipeline: How to Identify, Develop and Retain Leadership Talent.* San Francisco, CA: Jossey-Bass, 2001.

Collins, Jim. *Good to Great: Why Some Companies Make the Leap and Others Don't.* New York, NY: HarperCollins Publishers, 2001.

Cooperrider, David. *Appreciative Inquiry: Rethinking Human Organization Toward a Positive Theory of Change.* Champaign, IL: Stipes Publishing, 1999.

Cooperrider, David, and Diana Whitney. *Appreciative Inquiry: A Positive Revolution in Change.* San Francisco, CA: Berrett-Koehler Publishers, 2005.

Corporate Executive Board. "Closing the Performance Gap." Catalog No. CLC1W10HS. 2002.

Corporate Executive Board. "Employee Performance Improvement: Understanding Your Role as a Manager." Catalog No. TD11A8Q65. 2003.

Corporate Executive Board. "Hallmarks of Leadership Success." Catalog No. CLC11Q0U3L. 2003.

Corporate Executive Board. "Engaging Managers as Agents of Employee Development." Catalog No. TD11IMXNC. 2003.

Corporate Executive Board. "Driving Performance and Retention Through Employee Engagement." 2004.

Corporate Executive Board. "Unlocking the Full Value of Rising Talent." 2005.

Corporate Executive Board. "Leaders Who Develop Leaders." 2006.

Covey, Stephen. *The Seven Habits of Highly Effective People: Restoring the Character Ethic.* New York, NY: Simon and Schuster, 1989.

Depree, Max. *Leadership is an Art.* New York, NY: Doubleday, 1990.

Drucker, Peter. *The Effective Executive.* New York, NY: Harper Row, 1967.

Friedman, Thomas. *The World is Flat.* New York, NY: Farrar, Straus and Giroux, 2005.

Fulmer, Robert, and Jay Conger. *Growing Your Company's Leaders: How Great Organizations Use Succession Management to Sustain Competitive Advantage.* New York, NY: AMACOM, 2004.

George, Bill. *Authentic Leadership: Rediscovering the Secrets to Creating Lasting Value.* San Francisco, CA: Jossey-Bass, 2003.

Gladwell, Malcolm. *The Tipping Point: How Little Things Can Make a Big Difference.* Lebanon, IN: Little, Brown and Company, 2000.

Goldsmith, Marshall. *What Got You Here Won't Get You There: How Successful People Become Even More Successful.* New York, NY: Hachette Book Group, 2007.

Goldsmith, Marshall, Beverly Kay, and Ken Shelton. *Learning Journeys.* Palo Alto, CA: Davies-Black Publishing, 2000.

Hamel, Gary. *Leading the Revolution.* Boston, MA: Harvard Business Review Press, 2000.

Hamel, Gary. *What Matters Now: How to Win in a World of Relentless Change, Ferocious Competition, and Unstoppable Innovation.* San Francisco, CA: Jossey-Bass, 2012.

Hammond, Sue. *The Thin Book of Appreciative Inquiry.* Bend, OR: Thin Book Publishing Company, 1996.

Heath, Chip, and Dan Heath. *Switch: How to Change Things When Change Is Hard.* New York, NY: Crown Business Publishing, 2010.

Hunter, Jeremy. "The Forgotten Fundamental of Human Performance: Managing Attention in the Age of Overwhelm and Distraction." Dallas, TX: Corporate Learning Week, November 9, 2016.

Journal of American Medical Association. "Study of Health Care Quality of Local Hospitals in the U.S." www.ama-assn.org, 2017.

Kotter, John. *Leading Change.* Boston, MA: Harvard Business Review Press, 1996.

Kouzes, James, and Barry Posner. *The Leadership Challenge: How to Make Extraordinary Things Happen in Organizations.* San Francisco, CA: Jossey-Bass, 2002.

Kouzes, James, and Barry Posner. *Credibility: How Leaders Gain and Lose It, Why People Demand It.* San Francisco, CA: Jossey-Bass, 2003.

Kouzes, James, and Barry Posner. *A Leader's Legacy.* San Francisco, CA: Jossey-Bass, 2006.

LaFasto, Frank and Carl Larson. *When Teams Work Best: 6,000 Team Members and Leaders Tell What it Takes to Succeed.* Thousand Oaks, CA: Sage publications Inc., 2001.

Laurie, Donald. *The Real Work of Leaders: A Report From The Front Lines Of Management.* Cambridge, MA: Perseus Publishing, 2000.

Marquardt, Michael. *Leading with Questions: How Leaders Find the Right Solutions by Knowing What to Ask.* San Francisco, CA: Jossey-Bass, 2005.

Oakley, Ed, and Doug Krug. *Enlightened Leadership: Getting to the Heart of Change.* New York, NY: Fireside, 1991.

Partnership for Public Service. "The Best Places to Work in the Federal Government." www.bestplacestowork.org, 2016.

Peters, Tom and Robert H. Waterman, Jr. *In Search of Excellence: Lessons from America's Best Run Companies.* New York, NY: Harper & Row Publishers, 1982.

Pink, Dan. *Drive: The Surprising Truth About What Motivates Us.* New York, NY: Riverhead Books, 2011.

President's Management Agenda. www.whitehouse.gov. 2016.

Quinn, Robert. *Deep Change: Discovering the Leader Within.* San Francisco, CA: Jossey-Bass, 1996.

Quinn, Robert. *Change the World: How Ordinary People Can Accomplish Extraordinary Results.* San Francisco, CA: Jossey-Bass, 2000

Rand Corporation. "2016 Report on Patient Satisfaction with U.S. Health Care Providers." Santa Monica, CA, 2016.

Rutzick, Karen. "Employees keep training expectations to themselves." www.govexec.com, January 23, 2006.

Senge, Peter. *The Fifth Discipline: The Art and Practice of the Learning Organization.* New York, NY: Doubleday, 1990.

Sinek, Simon. *Start With Why: How Great Leaders Inspire Everyone to Take Action.* Savannah, GA: Portfolio Publishing, 2009.

Spreitzer, Gretchen, and Robert Quinn. *A Company of Leaders: Five Disciplines for Unleashing the Power in Your Workforce.* San Francisco, CA: Jossey-Bass, 2001.

Tichy, Noel, and Mary Anne Devanna. *The Transformational Leader: The Key to Global Competitiveness.* New York, NY: John Wiley and Sons, 1990.

Tichy, Noel, and Eli Cohen. *The Leadership Engine: How Winning Companies Build Leaders at Every Level.* New York, NY: Harper Collins Publishing, 1997.

Trinka, Jim. "Building Great Leadership at the IRS." *Industrial and Commercial Training.* Volume 36, No. 7, 2004.

Trinka, Jim. "What's a Manager To Do?" *Industrial and Commercial Training.* Volume 36, No. 7, 2004.

Trinka, Jim. "Great Leaders." *Leadership Excellence.* July, 2005.

Trinka, Jim. "What's a Manager To Do?" *Leadership Excellence.* September, 2005.

Trinka, Jim. "What Leaders Need To Do." *Federal Times.* May 22, 2006.

U.S Department of Veteran Affairs. Veteran Experience Office Survey. Washington, DC: www.va.gov. 2017.

U.S. Office of Personnel Management. "2016 Federal Employee Viewpoint Survey: Empowering Employees, Inspiring Change." Washington, DC: www.opm.gov/fevs. 2016.

Wallace, Les, and Jim Trinka. *A Legacy of 21st Century Leadership: A Guide for Creating a Climate of Leadership Throughout Your Organization.* Lincoln, NE: iUniverse Books, 2007.

Watkins, Michael. *The First 90 Days: Critical Success Strategies for New Leaders at All Levels.* Boston, MA: Harvard Business Review Press, 2003.

Wheatley, Margaret. *Leadership and the New Science: Discovering Order in a Chaotic World.* San Francisco: CA: Berrett-Koehler, 1999.

Whitney, Diana. *The Power of Appreciative Inquiry: A Practical Guide to Positive Change.* San Francisco, CA" Berrett-Koehler, 2003.

Wiseman, Liz. *Multipliers: How the Best Leaders Make Everyone Smarter.* New York, NY: Harper Collins Publishing, 2017.

Useem, Michael. *The Leadership Moment: Nine True Stories of Triumph and Disaster and Their Lessons for Us All.* New York, NY: Crown Business Publishing, 1999.

Yankelovitch, Daniel. *The Magic of Dialogue: Transforming Conflict Into Cooperation.* New York, NY: Simon and Schuster, 1999.

Zenger, Jack, and Joe Folkman. *The Extraordinary Leader: Truning Good Managers Into Great Leaders.* New York, NY: McGraw-Hill, 2002.

ABOUT THE AUTHOR
Jim Trinka – PhD

Jim Trinka is the Chief Learning Officer for the Office of Information and Technology (OI&T) within the Department of Veterans Affairs (VA). In this role, he develops, implements, and manages a comprehensive employee and leadership development program designed to create and sustain a high-performing OIT workforce to serve our Nation's Veterans. He is the primary advocate for transforming OI&T into a learning organization. Previously, Jim served as the Executive Director of the *Leading EDGE* Program to design, develop, and deliver a government-wide program to help senior executives improve government performance and face challenges of decreasing budgets, increasing workloads, and unprecedented complexity. Prior to Jim's appointment with VA, he was the Technical Training Director for the Federal Aviation Administration (FAA), where he oversaw the development and implementation of an integrated workforce plan to hire and train 17,000 new air traffic controllers and received an FAA Leadership Award for his efforts. Prior to the FAA, Jim served as the FBI's Chief Learning Officer and managed the prestigious FBI Academy, the National Academy for state and local law enforcement officers, the Center for Intelligence Training, and the Leadership Development Institute. He implemented training initiatives crucial to the FBI's efforts to strengthen its intelligence workforce, build on its counterterrorism expertise, and prepare agents to deal with future global threats. Prior to the FBI, Jim served as the IRS' Director of Leadership and Organizational Effectiveness and led development programs to new heights, which continue to serve as benchmarks for both public and private institutions. He began his government service with a distinguished 22-year career as a fighter pilot in the Air Force. Jim holds a doctorate degree in International Politics from The George Washington University and has authored numerous works on leadership development and political science.

You may contact the author, Jim Trinka, at JTrinka@cox.net or through the website www.SingatureResources.com.

www.ingramcontent.com/pod-product-compliance
Lightning Source LLC
Chambersburg PA
CBHW030843180526
45163CB00004B/1436